VANCOUVER SPECIAL

BURRARD INLET

1914
Komagata Maru

KITSILANO

4th Ave.

1997 APEC
Demonstrations
at UBC

MUSQUEAM 2

Richmo

WELCOME TO
VANCOUVER

5,000 ft

1 km

↑
N

ARSENAL
PULP PRESS

VANCOUVER

VANCOUVER SPECIAL

BY

CHARLES DEMERS

Arsenal Pulp Press
Suite 200, 341 Water Street
Vancouver, BC
Canada V6B 1B8
arsenalpulp.com

The publisher gratefully acknowledges the support of the Canada Council for the Arts and the British Columbia Arts Council for its publishing program, and the Government of Canada through the Book Publishing Industry Development Program and the Government of British Columbia through the Book Publishing Tax Credit Program for its publishing activities.

Book design by Information Office
Photography by Emmanuel Buenviaje
Editing by Susan Safyan and Michelle Simms

Efforts have been made to locate copyright holders of source material wherever possible. The publisher welcomes hearing from any copyright holders of material used in this book who have not been contacted.

A selection from *Dream City* by Lance Berelowitz appears in the essay "Nature." Copyright Douglas & McIntyre, 2005. Used by permission of Douglas & McIntyre.

A selection from *The Jade Peony* by Wayson Choy appears in the essay "Chinatown." Copyright Douglas & McIntyre, 1995. Used by permission of Douglas & McIntyre.

A selection from "Vancouver's 'Brand': Ski Bums or Green Brainiacs?" by Geoff Dembicki appears in the essay "Nature." Copyright Geoff Dembicki, 2009. Used by permission of the author.

A selection from *Stardust* by Bruce Serafin appears in the essay "Kitsilano." Copyright New Star Books, 2007. Used by permission of New Star Books.

A selection from *Vancouver: A Poem* by George Stanley appears in the Introduction. Copyright New Star Books, 2008. Used by permission of New Star Books.

Library and Archives Canada Cataloguing in Publication

Demers, Charlie, 1980–
Vancouver special / Charles Demers.

Includes bibliographical references and index.
ISBN 978-1-55152-294-4

1. Vancouver (B.C.). I. Title.

FC3847.35.D45 2009   971.1'33   C2009-905373-X

Printed and bound in Canada

For my wife, Cara, who doesn't ever want to move back to Toronto.

Acknowledgments

This book was inspired to an enormous degree by the wonderful Vancouver authors, artists, activists, advocates, pizza vendors, *et al.*, who've been mentioned throughout. Although I can't list you all again here, if you find your name in the book (and you aren't a serial killer or a right-wing billionaire or something), please know how much I appreciate what you've done to make this city what it is, as well as what you've done to enrich my understanding of it.

Thank you to all the Vancouver comics who let me use their brilliant, hilarious bits; they are among the sharpest observations of Vancouver's absurdity that I could have shared with readers. I strongly encourage those same readers to support the art form by going to see these comedians, and the other fine stand-ups the city has to offer, live.

I want to thank Shyla Seller, Susan Safyan, Michelle Simms, Brian Lam, Robert Ballantyne, and Janice Beley at Arsenal Pulp, a publisher whose books and authors I have long admired and am humbled to be included alongside. Derek Barnett's artful and exciting design ideas prompted me to try and write a book worthy of them, and I also have nothing but gratitude for Emmanuel Buenviaje for his tremendous photography.

Derrick O'Keefe was a patient, insightful reader of panicked first drafts; Tejpal Singh Swatch, Alexandra Zabjek, Dwayne Finlayson, and Andrea Pinochet-Escudero also offered helpful and encouraging notes along the way. Thanks to each of you. Thanks to Kevin Chong and David Beers. Thanks as well to my family members, especially Dad, Nick, and Auntie Heather, for the personal memories and family histories that you shared with me. Finally, for her unending patience, her encouraging (but always critical and intelligent) feedback, and her love (of both her adoptive city and her husband, of which at least the latter is deeply reciprocated), thank you to my Toronto-born-and-raised wife, Cara Ng, to whom this book is dedicated.

Introduction

Everybody's last stop,
refuge,
terminus,
lotus land,
Shangri-La,
Canaan,
utopia.
Paradise colonized.
Babylon unbound.

—Wayde Compton, Vancouver poet/historian, "Performance Bond"

A comedian can tell a lot about his own city from the permutations to his act when it's taken on the road, as well as from how the far-flung audiences react to it. A Vancouver comic accustomed to performing in front of crowds as ethnically diverse as a medieval Ottoman port city will find that the joke he has about his interracial, white-Asian relationship—a joke that's only funny to him and the hometown audience because the subject is so banal, such a non-event—counts for downright exotic, a contemporary *Guess Who's Coming to Dinner?* at a gig just three hours' drive from the T & T Supermarket in East Van. A joke about a gay brother's marriage normally told at a Yuk Yuk's two blocks from Davie Street, the main artery of western Canada's most celebrated rainbow district, elicits a slightly more cruel, less empathetic laugh from club patrons in the Interior or on the Prairies. Both those bits are mine, and those responses are to my act, but the experience isn't unique to me, nor is it simply an urban-versus-rural thing—one of Vancouver's youngest, most promising stand-ups once lamented to me his inability to connect with a Toronto crowd over a joke about homelessness. Even as he told me the story his face was all exasperation: why couldn't they get that it was *funny*, not *mean*?

Conversely, the rest of the country laps up jokes about stereotypical Vancouver, with its stock of potheads and its rain and its pussiness in the face of a boreal country's winters. One night, opening for Tommy Chong in Alberta, I shared my surprise with the audience at having learned that Tommy's hometown was

Calgary, not Vancouver, where he and Cheech had gotten their start performing their druggy schtick: "How can Tommy Chong not be from Vancouver?" I mock demanded. "He's half-white, half-Chinese, and high all the time. That could be the slogan on our license plates!" Each night, the Calgary audience loved it; the same line bombed every time I tried it at home.

This is not to say that we abhor clichés here in Vancouver. Among the many easy targets for stand-up comedians performing in Vancouver, the close-by, suburban municipality of Surrey with its ashy reputation for sprawl and track-pants and a brainless gangsterism more reminiscent of *Mean Streets* DeNiro than *Godfather* DeNiro—is the easiest. On a Friday or Saturday night at a club downtown, a joke at Surrey's expense sends a superior trill through the crowd like the bolt that runs through a sports arena during the wave. The Surrey Joke is, in fact, such a reliable standby that when Dana Carvey (of *Saturday Night Live* and *Wayne's World* and the classic *Master of Disguise*) performed at the Red Robinson Theatre in the summer of 2008, he was advised by a stagehand that the best way to win over the audience would be to mock the promiscuity of Surrey's fairer sex. In Carvey's case, the sure-thing apparently sputtered and died, which he lamented in an apologetic burlesque on Jay Leno's *Tonight Show* a few weeks later. The whole affair was covered on the popular Lower Mainland blog *Miss604.com*, which happens to be maintained by a Surrey native who had to close the comments section on the story for all the vitriol being heaped on her hometown. The Carvey incident is now, a year later, one more three-quarters-forgotten episode in the long relationship that Vancouver has had with American comedians, starting with Jack Benny (without whose fundraising efforts we wouldn't still have our beloved Orpheum,[i] the opulent site of innumerable orchestral performances as well as my high school graduation ceremony).

Some might be tempted to classify Vancouver's tortuously sophisticated anti-Surrey bias in the same category as Manhattan's disdain for the "bridge-and-tunnel-crowd," but the analogy isn't quite apt. In Manhattan, a genuine superiority complex is in play, making the contempt for peripheral suburbanites (in this case *sub*-urban, as in *beneath* city-dwellers) casual and off-handed. In provincial Vancouver, aspirant middle-class types desperately repeating the mantra world class city (that phrase being the closest

i. Thank you to Kliph Nesteroff for bringing this to my attention.

15

thing to a ritual prayer that we have out here) are so desperate not to be confused with the rubes east of Metrotown Mall that they lash out against Surrey with both vigour and fear. Not as important as Toronto, not as well-dressed as Montréal, not as rich as Calgary, Vancouver shits on Surrey like a kid with a lazy eye draws a bully's attention to the fat kid.

I had my own bout of Surreyitis in my late twenties when my father told me that I'd been wrong about the early parts of my biography. Because I was born at Surrey Memorial Hospital, and because my family had moved into my grandmother's South Burnaby home from a co-op in Newton, I had assumed that my first three years were spent in the suburb everybody loved to hate (although I knew we'd spent a little bit of time somewhere in Vancouver proper). But, Dad told me, my parents had brought me home from the hospital to the rented ground floor of a Vancouver Special[ii] on Kaslo Street in East Van, where we lived for the next two years. It was a made-in-Vancouver epiphany, like Paul on the 99 B-line to Damascus.

Retroactively, my family went from being lame-poor in our Newton co-op, to cool-poor, glamour-poor, *authentic*-poor with our thrillingly ethnic Portuguese landlords and Italian neighbours in East Van. Dad would take my stroller around the block in the summertime and come home drunk on homemade wine and grappa; our neighbours would leave buckets of backyard tomatoes on our windowsill; I would come back from my babysitter's with expensive new leather shoes from Commercial Drive, gifts from my honorific *nono* and *nona*.

We left East Van for Surrey because there'd been an opening for us in co-op housing; nearly thirty years later, my wife and I moved next to Trout Lake, just a few blocks from Kaslo Street, for the same reason. Not exactly Gatsbyian social mobility, but at least we're back in Vancouver.

> To see the sun through the murk of ideologies—
> pollution over the city, flows from west to east—
> is a haze indistinguishable from memory.

—George Stanley, from *Vancouver: A Poem*

This is a book of essays about Vancouver, written on the eve of the 2010 Winter Olympics by a Vancouverite who grew up with and

ii. A particular architectural style in Vancouver dating from roughly 1965 to 1985, characterised by a box-like shape, low-pitched roof, balcony across the front of the house, and brick or stone finish on the ground-floor level of the facade with stucco elsewhere.

after Expo 86, the Winter Games' traumatic, bookend precedent. Expo and the Olympics are the city's twin late-capitalist dislocations, each project brought about through the combined efforts of corporate hyperboosters and right-wing politicos (with help from social democratic converts to free marketeering), drawing money in from richer places and purging poverty into the streets to make room. Taken as a pair, they bring to mind Marx's phrase about history first as tragedy, then as farce: one of the earliest, leading opponents of the 2010 Games, who had the vision and far-sightedness to see what nobody else wanted to—the budget overruns, the mass evictions, the ecological devastation—was Chris Shaw, an opthamologist.

Nevertheless, Expo 86, which also marked Vancouver's centennial, is the most important experiential borderline in terms of how a Vancouverite sees and defines her city. For many affluent, market-oriented, and globalized cosmopolitans, Expo was the springboard from which we left the sleepy gravity of moribund, resource-extraction provincialism and threw our once-sinewy, lumberjack arms open to sushi and foreign investment. For critical nostalgics on both the right and left, 1986 is when the city all went to hell. From the plaid-and-corduroy progressives, the flak comes from Expo's place in the city's rhetorical and actual neo-liberal firmament. But it's not unusual to hear the paranoid, white remembrances of the city from racists who find all sorts of euphemistic ways (not) to say what they really mean: after Expo is when all the immigrants started coming—it's when the city became "Hongcouver." Less often, an imagined, pre-'86 city is invoked by those too young to remember it as part of articulating a vision of a better, more inclusive Vancouver, as when award-winning journalist Sean Condon, who edits the outstanding street newspaper *Megaphone*, waxed euphoric about "a balls out working class city [...] like Newfoundland, but on weed":

> It's hard to imagine that a city now known for its bloated real estate, yuppie cokeheads and inability to buy a beer, gave birth to bands like D.O.A. and the Subhumans and made Dave "Tiger" Williams a hockey star. If the Vancouver of 1980 met the Vancouver of 2008, it would give it a curbie. Not only would I go back to that time, I would take the rest of this city with me.[1]

But while a significant layer of Vancouverites can anecdotally weigh the pros and cons of the changes to their city since Expo, a growing number knows nothing but the geography of life after it (give or take a few years): the SkyTrain, Canada Place, Science World, BC Place, apartment and condominium towers along one side of False Creek, Granville Island on the other, the Inukshuk, big-city population, immigration from everywhere, NAFTA, and the sudden, assertive discovery that we are a Pacific Rim city. This is the only city known to those born here who are under thirty, but also—in a city where nearly half the population is foreign born— it's the only city known to those who arrived during the last major wave of immigration (an immigration fed by sources all around the globe, but especially by the exodus from Hong Kong in the lead-up to the Handover in 1997, which transferred sovereignty from Britain back to China) there's no overestimating the role that Expo played in shaping our imaginations: I can clearly remember my grade one teacher's frustrated attempts to explain to us one fall afternoon that, just because Expo 86 was over, it was not yet 1987. For those of us, young or from elsewhere—and there are a lot of us—the city as it is after a massive and fairly recent sea-change is the only one we can readily call to mind.

Of course, that's no excuse for amnesia. One of the foundational agreements of civic life is the commitment to a memory longer than a collection of personal anecdotes or family stories. A longer view of Vancouver's timeline can throw what might seem novel or unprecedented about today's city into sharp, historical relief. In looking at 2009's discussion about free speech zones and a city council bylaw against anti-Olympic signage during the Games, for instance, it's easy to see the analogy with the Industrial Workers of the World's free speech battle of 1912, centred around what is now Oppenheimer Park[2]—easy, provided you know that it happened (it might also inspire contemporary protestors to know that the IWW won). Similarly, massive dislocations of poor, working-class and, especially, Native people for recreational mega-projects like Expo and the Olympics are descended from the first such Vancouver endeavour, Stanley Park, which is nevertheless a wonder despite its brutal history. Actually, as far as city slogans go, Vancouver could do far worse than "Nevertheless a Wonder Despite its Brutal History!" The city's past is marked by the sometimes-successful attempt by

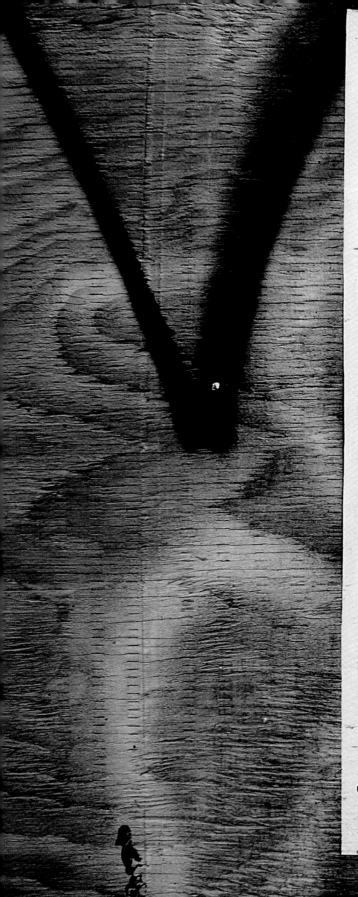

The Peo
v.s.
The City of

DTES Community

Sunday Apri.

Pigeon Park (Hastin

Food & drinks at 1pm - T

Accused	Charge	Date of Offense
The City of Vancouver	Social Cleansing	July 2003 - Present

Synopsis: Since the Olympic Bid of 2003 the City of Vancouver has waged a violent war on the community of the DTES.

*Street homelessness increased by 373% since 2002.

*Street Sweeps: Tickets for sitting or lying on the street & asking for spare change among other by law 'offenses.

*Brutalizaion & harassment by the VPD has reached deadly results

The City of Vancouver has literally criminalized the poverty it has created. It's time to fight for REAL justice

Organized by a collaboration of DTES com
organizers. With the support of: The
The Anti-Poverty Committee, SFPIRG, The

Vancouverites to create something meaningful, civil, democratic, and rewarding inside the strictures set by the agendas of states and corporations. At base, Vancouver really only exists because the Canada Pacific Railway bluffed the provincial government and smaller-fry local capitalists into giving it a massive land grant,[3] but that doesn't stop us from trying to have fun here. Just look at what a good time counter-culture Vancouver has had with the nickname Terminal City (whether the defunct alternative newspaper or the sexy grrrl roller-derby team) despite the fact that the phrase itself reduces the city to nothing more than a CPR company memo come to life. (Not to mention that it makes Vancouver sound like some sort of inoperable disease.)

But as author George Bowering said, we in Vancouver and BC don't live in history, "we live instead in geography." (Bowering also, in a novel about George Vancouver, gave an eighteenth-century Indian chief the line, "In the winter, it rains all the time, but we always say that at least you don't have to shovel it,"[4] which, if it isn't the best thing ever written about Vancouver, it's close). Long memories don't go well with either consumerist or colonial-settler societies, and Vancouver's both, often at the same time. Especially when we're skiing. My own first memories of the city are as a six-year-old at Expo, thrilled with nearly everything about it besides the height restrictions that kept me off the Scream Machine, a deadly cool roller coaster that Wikipedia tells me is now at Six Flags in St Louis and goes by the name Ninja (it's rare that something leaves Vancouver and becomes *more* Asian). Too young to know about the Socreds or Jimmy Pattison, I was simply taken with the whole affair, the compiled scenes of which have simmered down in my mind to a memorial reduction of the film *Colour Wars*; the monorail, those neat wire benches, and the wavy grey strip with all the cars on it. Years later, when I was eighteen and a Trotskyist and working for the summer at the Scott Paper factory in New Westminster, I got to spend time in what had been the Soviet Union's Expo pavilion before it was purchased by the paper tiger to add to its sprawling premises next to the SkyTrain line.

But even without the leap from personal to social memory, my roots in this city go back further than Expo. In a town famous for being populated entirely by folks from elsewhere, I can make the rare claim to have not only been born here to a mother who was born here, but to having *both* maternal grandparents born here. Among Vancouver's non-Musqueam-or-Squamish population, this is equivalent to being descended from one of the naked babies in the clam under the raven in Bill Reid's sculpture (of which, while I'm on the subject: Teachers, please stop taking little kids to see that thing until they're old enough to appreciate it as art and as religion; all I could concentrate on were the babies' balls).

My mom's mom and dad were both born in 1925, the same year construction ended on the Second Narrows Bridge connecting Vancouver to the North Shore. Granny's parents were working-class Britons who had been living in Seattle until they learned they were expecting a child; they came to Vancouver to raise their family in the Realm, and my great-grandfather found work in a foundry. My grandfather's dad, Alexander Birnie, was the déclassé scion of an ultra-wealthy Scottish merchant family whose patriarch punished thirteen-year-old Alexander by signing him on to a ship when he refused to go to boarding school. He sailed around the world until he was in his thirties, and his adventures around the treacherous Cape Horn were a point of particular familial pride during my childhood in South Burnaby, just up the hill from the Chinese farms on the Fraser River. Alexander, too, came to Vancouver via America, in his case Wyoming.

My grandparents, Florence and Ronald, grew up together in Fraserview, the neighbourhood where in 2009 an explosive electoral battle between two Legislature candidates of Asian descent, a high-profile Chinese-Canadian journalist and the first-ever Indo-Canadian police chief in the country, was fought over drug decriminalization and inaccurate English-to-Cantonese translation. My grandparents were in their twenties by the time Asians could vote here and the city had its first marijuana prosecution. They went to John Oliver Secondary together until my Granny left to study hairdressing at the technical high school, Van Tech (coincidentally, my widowed Granny was later briefly married to Raymond Hennessey, of Vancouver salon and beauty-school fame, and the only person I ever sensed that my abundantly generous mother actually hated). Granny, in whose house I lived along with my parents, my brother, and my aunt, worked most of her professional life at Pacific Press, Vancouver's peculiar two-newspaper monopoly[iii], an empire put together with what in the early

iii. According to Marc Edge, the only major city to have both rival papers owned by the same company.

twentieth century had been the city's Conservative and Liberal mouthpieces, the *Province* and the *Sun*, respectively. Growing up, even after Granny retired, we always got both papers; when I was a kid, the *Sun* was actually fairly decent, and the *Province* was only as bad as the *Sun* is now. Her stories about Pacific Press were fascinating, and usually told with eye-rolled exasperation about male behaviour—particularly her feeling that the typesetters were showing off by the way that they would read their books and newspapers upside down, or her insistence that food columnist James Barber (who became CBC's rightly beloved *Urban Peasant*) would wear filthy sandals in to work like a dirty hippie.

My dad's relationship to the city is more like the immigrant norm: in the mid-1970s, my francophone father and his friend Louis left the suburbs of Montréal on a summer vacation hitchhiking across the country to see Louis's sister on the West Coast. Louis hated everything about Vancouver and headed back almost immediately; my dad felt immediately at home in the city and stayed.

Years later, my little brother and I were introduced to the great potential of Vancouver architecture at Simon Fraser University, where my dad studied to become a teacher. Though I would grow to appreciate Arthur Erickson's campus with slightly greater sophistication (I went to school there for four years and didn't need an umbrella! In *Vancouver*!), the main feature of his design that we noticed as kids was that if you dragged your toes on the floors of the academic quadrangle it sounded like you were farting. During his studies, Dad worked part-time as a dispatcher for the Burnaby RCMP, which put him in touch with several incidences of Lower Mainland history: he took the emergency calls for the Oakalla prison break as well as for the notorious collapse of the rooftop parking lot into the newly opened Save-On-Foods at Station Square (which temporarily earned the BC institution the sobriquet "Cave-On Foods").

My mother grew up here and married someone who came from one of the cities Vancouverites are envious of, but who himself fell in love with Vancouver. A generation later, I did the same thing: my wife, Cara, comes from Toronto and refuses ever to move back. This was once a problem for me, since as a writer and comedian, it made little economic sense for me to be here in Vancouver, "Hollywood North" notwithstanding.

Luckily, having stuck it out, I fell miraculously into a job at Citytv. Though it's now owned from Toronto, the station, whose call letters are CKVU, was once the locally owned broadcaster where the *Vancouver Show* and *Vancouver Live* were produced. I'm lucky enough to work every day with editors, cameramen, and floor directors who made broadcasting history in the city I love and hope never to have to leave for too long.

So here's a book about the city written on the eve of major changes that, very possibly, will shift the realities recorded herein, though not likely beyond recognition. Even at the rate at which things turn over in this town, Vancouver works in echoes of itself, as well as with the seemingly permanent tendencies explored in these pages. This collection of essays considers the themes and histories and features of Vancouver, its neighbourhoods and recent trends and sundry civic idiosyncrasies: buck-a-slice pizza, for example, or the whole Vancouver dog obsession. I've also included reflections on some of the phenomena I feel have been a part of Vancouver throughout its history: anti-Asian racism, for instance, or the city's history of anarchism.

Finally, sown throughout the text are bits from some of Vancouver's finest stand-up comedians—talking about Vancouver. For the past five years I've had the pleasure of being part of a frighteningly talented community of comic artists, working the city for virtually no money and recognition that largely comes only from outside. Celebrated American comic Zach Galifianakis—who lived here while filming a Fox television B-series called *Tru Calling*, and who was a regular at Commercial Drive's alternative comedy nights at the El Cocal—once observed that Vancouver comedy had the potential to develop into something as unique as Seattle music.[iv] Some of the sharpest, funniest minds in the world are at work in this city, as should be obvious from the way they've nailed Vancouver in the bits included here. Maybe if we can have a good laugh about ourselves, we can finally cut Surrey some slack.

iv. Thank you to *Georgia Straight* comedy writer Guy MacPherson for providing these notes.

Every now and again, shifting plates from the various, sedimentary layers of Commercial Drive's social geology bump up against each other; the results are rarely seismic, and they can be fun to watch. Such was the case when a lactose-intolerant Drive-type weaned on sprouty vegan restaurants perfectly attuned to the intricacies of food allergies sidled up to the counter of Café Roma, an Italian sports-and-coffee bar where old men play cards and there was once, for a little while, a cut-out image of the cast of *The Sopranos* tacked up behind the till.

"Oh," said the patron, watching horrified as the old Italian heaped a spoonful of steamed milk on top of his drink. "I can't have dairy."

The old man sighed, shook his head, and creased his face into a casual go-fuck-yourself as he poured out the drink and started afresh.

"Yeah, sorry," said the patron with wincing ingratiation. "I didn't know you were going to put milk on it."

"I'm not a magician," said the old Italian. "I can't read your mind." What I loved most was his choice of the word "magician," as though it wouldn't take supernatural powers to divine what a coffee drinker wanted, but just the sweaty effort devoted to something demeaning like card tricks or customer service.

Commercial Drive is a long, north-south street much narrower than most major thoroughfares in the city, a fact that has engendered a pathological culture of jaywalking that turns the two sides of the road into a piazza. Vancouver's much-celebrated Car-Free Day festivals, when huge blocks of major roads are shut down to automotive traffic and opened to various commercial, cultural, and political community activities, got started on the Drive, a place that barely needed to make such an event official.

While other Vancouver neighbourhoods change drastically from generation to generation, no group has ever really left the Drive after settling there, no matter how incongruous the next wave of settlers. This has created a sort of swirling collection of partial hegemons (a bit of a nod to Gramsci, who is at the very least Italian). The Drive's Big Three groups, if there were ever a Yalta summit with the street's Stalin, Churchill, and Roosevelt, are the Italians, the Lesbians, and the Leftists (the dykes and commies are Winston and Franklin here because of their close alliance; the Italians aren't Stalin for any political reason, just the moustache and the shared tendency of Soviet leaders and Mediterraneans to decorate their chests with shiny medals). Along with the Big Three are various independent constituencies (the hipsters, the Natives, the Afro hair salons and Caribbean restaurants, the spoken word poets) as well as satellites of the great powers (the Portuguese, the hippies, the vegetarians).

The resulting blue-collar Bohemian compound seemed like a miracle to me and my friends during our last years of high school; unpopular and unfucked, we were a quartet of young Trotskyists whose revolutionary and intellectual pretensions were, incredibly, redeemed by a simple twenty-minute drive from Burnaby out to La Quena, a collective-run, insurrectionary coffee shop where we could eat vegan brownies the consistency and flavour of topsoil and argue with middle-aged First Nations Maoists about whether or not the working class American soldiers who had been in Vietnam deserved whatever they got. La Quena had been founded in the early 1980s by hard-left exiles from Pinochet's Chile (the father of one of my best friends among them); over the years the controlling body morphed into a broader, more diverse group dedicated to Central American solidarity more generally. By the time we got there, long after the glory days but just before it went to seed, a more anarchist tendency was running things. Today, you still run into leftists just recovering from the drama of the café's last years, but my friends and I loved it right up until our politics became more rigidly codified in their sectarian ways; after that, we couldn't appreciate the thousand flowers blooming. Today, the building that used to house La Quena is a yoga studio.

Across and slightly south of La Quena was, and still is, Joe's Café, eponymously named for its owner, who can best be physically described as a tall, Latin leprechaun (and I mean tall for a leprechaun; Joe's regular-sized, but there's something shamrocky about that face). My friends and I played endless games of twenty-five-cent foosball on Joe's ratty tables (the café's aesthetic was proletarianized Europa; as much duct tape as Ducati), vaguely aware of the gay-rights standoff that had rocked the place a few years earlier in September 1990.

By the time we came along, the Joe's Café standoff was mythical, the factual kernel of its origins buried deep in conflicting stories. Some had it that a sweet, rosy-cheeked lesbian couple had shared a virginal peck and been thrown out into the street by a red-faced Joe

pledging his eternal allegiance to Salazar and calling in Bull Connor's Birmingham police with their hoses; others told it differently, with two sweating, pulsating dykes grinding their jaws and crotches into each other like drunk college kids while confused-immigrant Joe, head bowed, straight from Ellis Island, and still holding his violin and choleric baby, had politely tapped one of them on the shoulder and asked in broken English if they wouldn't be more comfortable in the bridal suite. The funniest by-product of the standoff was a painted exchange on the side of Joe's building: a vandal scrawled the phrase "Salazar was gay" on to the wall, where it was still partially visible even after Joe had it painted over it with a rainbow.

The most compelling version of the gay-rights standoff at Joe's— not the Kiss itself, but the context and the aftermath—comes from the wonderful and, tragically, late Vancouver writer Bruce Serafin, a former postal worker who also published *Vancouver Review* and two books of essays, including *Colin's Big Thing*, a memoir whose sharp and melancholic prose brings Commercial Drive to just as vivid, if starkly more sombre, a life as St Urbain enjoys in Mordecai Richler's collection *The Street*. (The Drive has been immortalized in print by others as well: most terrifyingly by Eden Robinson in *Blood Sports*; most hauntingly and ethereally by George Stanley in *Vancouver: A Poem*; most lovingly by Ivan E. Coyote in much of her work.) In a moment slightly over-brimming with Vancouverismo, I got turned on to Serafin's book by Matt Bryant, the lead singer of local folk music quartet Headwater, while we sat in a bar on Commercial watching the Canucks blow a playoff lead.

The fight at and over Joe's is the centrepiece of Serafin's brilliantly pessimistic essay "Joe's Beach." Cast as a pale provincial aping of Spike Lee's searing urban drama *Do the Right Thing*, which came out just before the incident, the essay also focused on the *kulturkampf* between a Romantic petit bourgeois and his socially marginalized clientele. Primarily, though, Serafin used the controversy as an encapsulation of the militant self-righteousness—what he lamented as the "walled-off mentality" of the Drive—that he saw taking over the neighbourhood, captured especially in the esoteric political graffiti that he noticed rather suddenly after returning home from a trip to the Interior. Reading "Joe's Beach" fills me with a certain amount of guilt, because the same shrill, left-wing stridency that so turned him off was precisely what drew me and my friends in. Serafin wrote of overconfident university students trying to construct the neighbourhood around themselves, and maybe I've never been as bothered as he was because my friends and I were just the Little Archie versions of the snots he saw undermining the civility of the Drive.

Serafin's piece is a stark corrective in perceiving a neighbourhood that's easy to get giddy about. For many of the people in Vancouver who complain about the placid provincialism, the sometimes almost-suburban quality the city, the Drive is the exceptional case, the strip of our outsized suburb that most resembles Montréal or New York or someplace in Europe with cobblestones and bikes and civilized drug laws (for a while we even had a storefront pot dealer a few feet from the elementary school). The Drive is like a neighbourhood in an older, more sophisticated city, where it's the poor people who are left-wing and a certain particulate violence sort of hangs in the air. And yet still there's something uniquely Vancouver about the Drive: the patio seating at Havana before winter's finished, the anarchists playing bicycle polo at Grandview Park.

It seems to me that a lot of what Serafin saw as wrong with the Drive has worked itself out, at least temporarily. These days, the youngish, student impulse on Commercial is more hipster than *Utne Reader* reader, and for the new young men and women, the snap-button, Dickies-wearing Southern Europeans picking up tools from the Home Hardware are not an obstacle to the Drive's cultural cache, but rather a necessary component of it. Today's self-righteousness is far more likely to be the self-righteous defence of a neat, throwbacky kind of layer epitomized in a divey place like Joe's; Serafin had it that Joe's before the boycott had "perfectly suited the Drive's fantasy of an environment that was simultaneously street-tough and politically correct," but now that sort of political correctness might be seen as fatally inauthentic (you never see rainbow flags in Scorsese films).

For its part, strident leftism has mellowed into the mix more comfortably, with greater security and less self-consciousness, and is part of a cultural chemistry that would be hard to eradicate through gentrification because it's such a large part of what draws would-be gentrifiers to the neighbourhood in the first place. Sure, there are certain real-world, on-the-ground, infrastructural realities that keep the yuppie beachheads between Commercial and

Victoria Drive from taking over completely: too much Native social housing, too many housing co-ops, too many renters of shitty places in ugly buildings, too many drug dealers, and too many SkyTrain stations for the upwardly mobile with their babies (and mobiles) to ever wholly remake the neighbourhood in their image. But the thing is, the *kinds* of yuppies who move to the Drive generally don't want to remake it anyway; the culture of the place is thorough-going and established and charming. Contrarily, Serafin wrote:

> [T]he atmosphere had been changed by my generation of militants and the students and bohemians who had arrived in their wake. By and large they were animated not so much by a love of the neighbourhood as by a resentment of everything that surrounded it. This resent-ment—so often, for the older militants, fuelled by a sense of personal failure—was a powerful force; and it had led to a garrison mentality on the Drive.[5]

I could be wrong, but I don't think anybody would write that of Commercial today. The Drive is increasingly a culturally valued, sought-out geography. But unlike the young people drawn to the blocks between the teens and twenties on Main Street to create a new neighbourhood whole cloth, those drawn to Commercial Drive want to be part of what's already there.

So of all the neighbourhoods in Vancouver, the Drive is the hardest one to describe without slipping into unabashed romanti-cism; but why resist it? When my wife and I got married, one of the nicest parts was the absolute integration of our neighbourhood into the wedding (we were living at First and Victoria): my suit was tailored on the Drive by Angelo, a man so short he practi-cally had to lift his arms above his head to measure my waist; the flowers came from a shop kitty-corner to Grandview Park; the coffee was gifted to us by Nick at Continental Coffee, who makes the best latte on the street; the dinner was cooked for us at cost by the head chef of Rime, a now sadly defunct Turkish restaurant; the ceremony and reception both took place at the WISE Hall, the Welsh-Irish-Scottish-English bar/auditorium on Adanac Street just past Venables. After I put on my suit, my father, my brother, one of my best friends, and I walked to the WISE Hall in the December sun,

taking in the street as we made our way down Commercial. Today my wife and I are constantly surrounded by pleasant reminders of the wedding, infused as it was by a neighbourhood that, at its best, works like a marriage is supposed to: cobbling together the disparate, sometimes antagonistic, sometimes sublimely harmonic into something sweet, exciting, and comfortable at once.

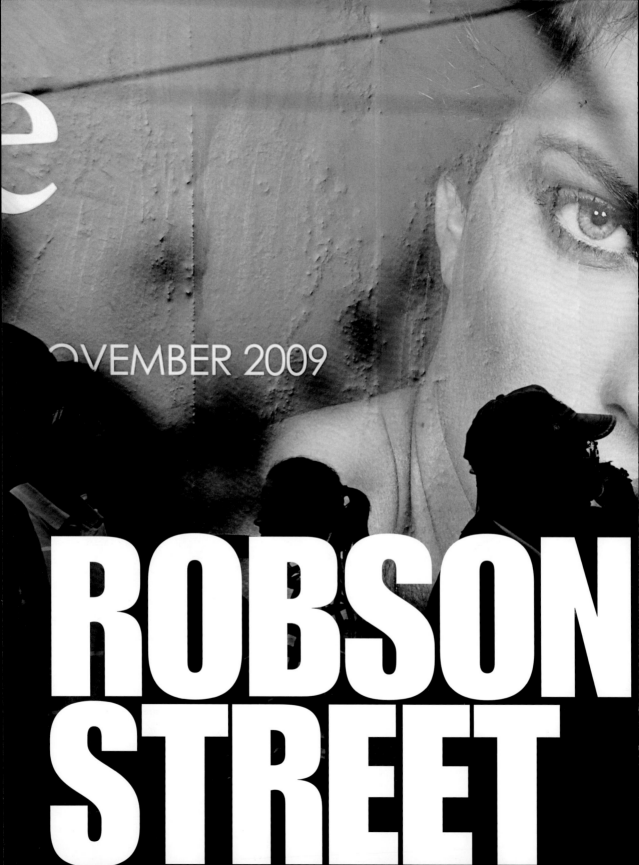

Of all the tricks played by fate and oligarchy to make political radicals feel small, isolated, and insecure, none worked quite so well as situating Vancouver's only central, transit-served, open, public gathering space in the middle of Robson Street. The steps of the Vancouver Art Gallery have been the site of countless rallies against any number of brutalities, demonstrations almost invariably followed by marches along the world-renowned lineup of luxury

I LOVE VANCOUVER: THE MOUNTAINS, THE OCEAN, THE DAILY DEBILITATING FEAR OF AN EARTHQUAKE SWALLOWING US WHOLE. AND I DON'T HAVE ANY SERIOUS COMPLAINTS— HOWEVER, I THINK WOMEN IN VANCOUVER SHOULD TRY TO EMBRACE INDIVIDUAL STYLE A BIT MORE, BECAUSE WHEN THE BIG ONE HITS, AND IT WILL ANY DAY NOW, IT'S GOING TO BE VERY DIFFICULT FINDING OUR LOVED ONES IF EVERYONE IS STILL WEARING LULULEMON TRACK SUITS. THERE WILL JUST BE PILES OF BODIES ON THE SIDE OF THE ROAD STACKED LIKE FIREWOOD, BLACK TRACKSUITS, UGG BOOTS, AND OVER-PROCESSED BLONDE HAIR, AND AS THE DAYS WEAR ON, YOU ARE JUST GOING TO HAVE TO PICK ONE AND BURY IT.

ALICIA TOBIN

shops that draws and keeps tourists and rich folks like a long strip of fly tape. Once a march starts, each of the two constituencies—the earnest, angry protesters, the hapless, apolitical consumers—either tries to ignore the other or stares openly, with incomprehension and more than a little disdain, as though each were taking the other in through a one-way mirror.

Usually, a few demonstrators attempt to break through the cordon—sometimes sweetly (asking if passers-by would like a pamphlet), sometimes confrontationally (as with the awful, shrill chant that has gained some popularity on Robson, "While you're shopping, bombs are dropping!"; it is difficult, if not impossible, to imagine anybody being inspired by this to drop their bag of shoes and commit themselves to the cause of global justice). The feeling from inside the demonstration is one of being sealed off from the general population, moving through it exotically, like the wax in a

lava lamp rising through the water. Derrick O'Keefe, the anti-war activist, author, and journalist, summed up the discordant inter-section of the two groups on Robson during Israel's 2006 invasion of Lebanon. Derrick found himself handing out leaflets on the peripheries of the crowd of protestors, trying to run one of the aforementioned Hail Mary efforts to connect with shoppers.

"Some information against war?" he asked a blonde woman walking a poodle alongside her tall, handsome, dark-haired boyfriend.

"War?" she asked. "*Psh*. I *support* war."

"You know what," countered Derrick, his patience vaporized instantly, "Why don't you just fuck off with your Chris-Isaak look-alike douchebag." The boyfriend—who was, in fact, Chris Isaak[v]—was duly shocked (actually, given that it was Chris Isaak, he was probably dully shocked).

v. *The Chris Isaak Show* used to be filmed in Vancouver; did you ever see it? I didn't.

Although you would never be able to tell by looking at it now, Robson Street was, relatively recently in its history, an eclectic street with a strong Euro-Bohemian streak. When we were little kids, growing up in the 1980s, my brother and I would play a game called "Count the Weirdos" every time our family drove up Robson; as we rode in the back seat of the car, we would keep a running tab of every punk we saw, for example, wearing a massive, multi-coloured Mohawk and a leather bomber with no shirt. I mention

our retrospectively close-minded and mean-spirited little game for two reasons: First, because it shows how much things can change and how fast—today's sea of identical, luxuriously dressed Robson pedestrians would probably be the last crowd in the city in which Vancouver kids would hope to catch a glimpse of renegade style and aggressive idiosyncrasy. And second, it's the closest thing that I have in the banks of my personal memory to scientific data related to the transformation of Vancouver's most famous street. Just like a fisherman who can describe the degradation of a particular river by telling stories of his dwindling steelhead catches, I can distinctly remember my childhood disappointment as Robson weirdo-counts went from the high water mark of the mid-twenties for a single ride, down to the upper teens, before slowing to almost nothing. The last time I had the heart to play, when I was on the cusp of puberty but the street was already well into its change, the count was a paltry four and almost all sightings concentrated around the steps of the art gallery (even today, thankfully, weirdo-hunters can visit the game preserve on the gallery's steps, which still attract a healthy sample of stoners and punks who are somehow invisible before they cross Hornby or Howe only to appear again on the block in between).

For a street whose very recent history seems so remote, Robson's story goes back a long way. In his jolly narration of the Vancouver Historical Society's reissues of William Harbeck's 1907 film of Vancouver, Jim McGraw points out the concrete sidewalks already lining what was then a residential street and describes the construction of the Manhattan apartment building at Robson and Thurlow as "one of the first multi-family dwellings" the city ever saw.[6] A September 1983 *Province* article about the salvaging of the building (it had just become, and still remains, a housing co-operative) opens with style: "A posh residential address, a place to be seen dining, a hippie hangout, an anti-demolition protestors' squatting grounds— the Manhattan Building at Robson and Thurlow has been all these things."[7] For a brief period in the mid-1970s (during the building's "hippie hangout" phase), my father lived in the building; today, what he remembers most are the cage doors of the elevator.

My dad's then-brand-new English wouldn't likely have been much of a stumbling block back then, because the street was (as it is now, in one of Robson's few comforting bits of continuity) a mecca for immigrants. As McGraw explains in his narration, the post-

World War II period on Robson was marked by so much European immigration that it became known colloquially as Robsonstrausse. Today, the immigration has shifted decidedly away from Europe in favour of Asia, and instead of delis, you get shops like Konbiniya (otherwise known as the Pocky Store for its huge, Glico Pocky signs out front), with every conceivable Japanese snack on the ground floor and a karaoke lounge upstairs. The best karaoke bar in Vancouver, Fantacity, is also just off Robson, a short walk down Thurlow from the Manhattan.

When my brother and I were little, my dad often brought us to the ground floor of the building where he used to live to visit Manhattan Books, which had a wide range of French books and periodicals, as well as Tintin comics (a bookstore owned by the legendary Duthies, which sold their non-English titles and publications). The Manhattan bookstore was breathtaking. Set on two levels, it felt otherworldly to me even then, like it should be in an older, more cosmopolitan city—like somehow I knew it would be taken away (today it's a jewellery store).

The sophistication of those visits, the foreign-language newspapers lining the walls on the ground floor of a dignified Edwardian building, seems incredibly remote now. Certainly, I'm remembering them with a degree of undue romance, as though they were part of a better, smarter past; the Manhattan was still there in 1994 when the intersection gave birth to one of Vancouver's most bone-headed outpourings of hooliganism, the Stanley Cup riots. But it takes one hell of a fall from grace for *that* not to be the most embarrassing thing about an intersection.

Instead, the intersection of Robson and Thurlow is most notorious for being the home of Vancouver's kitty-corner Starbucks, the yuppy idiocy of which were immortalized by Parker Posey and Michael Hitchcock, playing the horrible *bourgeoises* Meg and Hamilton Swan in Christopher Guest's *Best in Show* (filmed in Vancouver). As Meg and Hamilton tell the story of how they met—noticing each other from across the street, each in his own Starbucks, then each going to the opposite one to meet the other— audiences all around the world laughed. Knowing exactly where the improv actors had been inspired, Vancouverites winced.

All this yuppy-bashing feels a bit like making a straw-man argument: even though it has lost most of its groove, there are still

pockets of interest on Robson—mostly in some of the best Korean, Japanese, and Chinese eateries in town. I'm not trying to draw a caricature of Robson Street—but there are plenty of guys along Robson who will draw a caricature of *you*, if you like. They're mostly older, Asian men sitting low to the sidewalk, pencils in hand. They're usually also selling charcoal drawings of Bob Marley and, almost always, Al Pacino as Tony "Scarface" Montana. The Scarface-on-Robson-Street phenomenon has never made any sense to me; if Tony is hoping to "kill a communist for fun," he's in the wrong part of the city. He'll have to wait until the next protest comes through, and keep his eyes out for someone who looks isolated and ill at ease.

CHINATO

One of the city's oldest neighbourhoods, Chinatown is so packed with history that the Vancouver Police Museum is currently involved in a project to develop an iPhone application that will use GPS to retrieve vice-squad stories from the city's early history along a particularly notorious strip of Pender Street. I mention the VPM's Sins of the City tour in the chapter on crime in Vancouver (see page 178), but the museum's executive director, Chris Mathieson, was

I USED TO BE A SOCIAL STUDIES TEACHER IN VANCOUVER. IT WAS A GREAT JOB. THE ONLY PROBLEM WAS WE HAD NO BUDGET SO I HAD TO WORK WITH REALLY OLD TEXTBOOKS. IN FACT, ONE TEXTBOOK WAS SO OLD THAT IT ACTUALLY SAID, "WHILE VANCOUVER IS A MULTICULTURAL CITY, THERE ARE RELATIVELY FEW CHINESE PEOPLE." I THOUGHT TO MY SELF, "WHAT? EITHER THIS IS A REALLY OLD TEXTBOOK, *OR*, IT'S A REALLY *SCARY* TEXTBOOK FROM THE FUTURE!" DAMN YOU BIRD FLU, YOU GOT US.

JEFF YU

formerly the Education Coordinator at Sun Yat-sen Garden, and so when it's his turn to lead the tour, the section on Chinatown is particularly muscular. Mathieson knows the neighbourhood well, and he's so confident of its fascinating properties that he unhesitatingly blows the air of mystique off of one of its greatest legends—turns out there are no tunnels under Chinatown—while outlining what *is* true and remarkable about the area: that it's a time capsule for Chinese traditions wiped out by the Cultural Revolution and a century of change in China; that it's full of hidden and false alleys, some of which hide courtyards that, even today, are like amber preserves of old Vancouver; that the Canton architecture, with its recessed balconies, are designed so that you can sit outside even when it rains (a trick that makes it seem even more natural and inevitable that the Chinese should end up here). He points out the Chinese Freemasons Hall at Pender and Carrall, where Dr Sun Yat-sen stayed on his several visits to Vancouver.[vi] The building's "Pekin Chop Suey" signage was recently found underneath layers of paint and is now legible once again, and highlights the building's

vi. Mathieson's Sins of the City Tour is not to be missed. The information he provided very much informed this essay, plus it made for a great afternoon.

富陶陶酒家

FOO'S HO HO RESTAURANT

102 EAST PENDER   ☎(604)609-2889

SIGN BY PEN-IN-HAND ☎ (604)874-9022 (12th Ave. & Commercial Dr.)

hybrid features: a recessed balcony, Canton-style on the Chinatown side of the building, Italianate on the Gastown side.

Chinatown's conservatism in recent years—which has at times been an unseemly, victim-blaming enterprise, opposed to many progressive drug-treatment initiatives—becomes a bit more understandable in light of the neighbourhood's long history of besiegement. Some communities come by their persecution complexes honestly, and if Chinatown thinks that the rest of the city is trying to destroy it or use it as a convenient site to offload social problems, it may just be because in the past, that has been true. That doesn't make today's NIMBYism right, but it certainly makes it understandable.

Jen Sookfong Lee's novel *The End of East* goes a long way toward capturing some of the claustrophobia, loneliness, and vulnerability of Vancouver's first Chinese settlers, and the musty, mouldy neighbourhood to which they were confined. In one of Vancouver's defining novels, *The Jade Peony*, Wayson Choy illustrates the suffocating dread and stranded despair of migrant workers cut off from home by the vicissitudes of racist policy making:

> Poverty-stricken bachelor-men were left alone in the Gold Mountain, with only a few dollars left to send back to China every month, and never enough dollars to buy passage home. Dozens went mad; many killed themselves. The Chinatown Chinese call July 1st, the day celebrating the birth of Canada, the Day of Shame [...] They had been deserted by the railroad companies and betrayed by the many labour contractors [...] China men were shoved aside, threatened, forgotten.[8]

The physical attacks on Chinatown, especially in the 1907 Riot, as well as the laws aimed against its residents and their families, contributed to the sense of being under siege. Decades later—barely twenty years after neighbouring Japantown had been ethnically cleansed by World War II internment—the city's twin mantras of "slum clearance" and "highway construction" threatened to flatten Chinatown once and for all.

Today, Vancouver's Chinese community is too large, well-dispersed, and well-established to seem exotic or out of place, even in a city founded on racism against them (although Chinese supporters of Vision Vancouver leadership candidate Raymond Louie claimed to have been targeted for unfair scrutiny and hoop-jumping at the party's nomination meeting in 2008). Mathieson points out that historic Chinatown is competing with a new "Chinatown," in Richmond. The proliferation of T & T Supermarkets throughout the city and its suburbs, the Crystal Mall in Burnaby and Aberdeen Mall in Richmond, as well as the increasing influence of East Asian communities on "mainstream" market centres like Pacific Centre and Metrotown, or even the food choices available at Save-On-Foods and Safeway, have all presented existential threats to Chinatown—slower-creeping, but in the end just as potentially dangerous, as the threats of the past.

Luckily, Chinatown has a deeper sense of history than any neighbourhood in Vancouver, with the tenacity that comes with 125 or so years of having to fight for itself. In May 2009, city-beat journalist and blogger Frances Bula posted an entry to her website titled "Mere suggestion of towers in Chinatown brings out the forces," describing the outcry and community turnout to oppose even the theoretical discussion of a high-rise next to the Sun Yat-sen Gardens.[9] Vancouver, a city that seems increasingly unwilling to stand up for itself or its history against developers and the slow creep of indifference respectively, could learn a lot from one of its oldest, most put-upon quarters.

As dedicated as anyone to the history of Vancouver's Chinatown is community organizer, amateur historian, and dragon boat coach Todd Wong, progenitor of Gung Haggis Fat Choy, a hybridized, annual celebration of what are arguably Vancouver's two most significant settler cultures, the Chinese and the Scottish. Gung Haggis has grown into a major Chinatown event; for the 2009 dinner, then newly elected Mayor Gregor Robertson cut the haggis. Wong—whose family goes as far back in this city as any non-Salish one can—took advantage of the chronological proximity between Chinese New Year and Robbie Burns Day to highlight a quintessentially Vancouver admixture.

Wong's dinner is still among the only places where Vancouver's Chinese history stands balanced with its British one. On CBC's *The Debaters,* in a comedy argument between two immigrants about the ease of assimilating, Scotland-born Al Rae told Korea-born Paul Bae that acculturating was easy; Bae retorted that Rae had moved from a country called Scotland to one with a province called *New* Scotland. Similarly, British settlers have been more naturalized in a place called British Columbia (which is a reason why, in one of his poems, Wayde Compton proposed a different set of possible names, including "Chinese Columbia").[10] Even after all this time, though they developed right alongside each other, somehow Gastown, despite its own multicultural pedigree, seems less exotic than Chinatown. Although it may be counterintuitive to think that haggis-filled wontons would make it seem *less* otherworldly, Wong appears to be banking on it.

KITSILAN

10

Visiting the Naam—Vancouver's "oldest natural foods restaurant,"[11] and one of the last real vestiges of the era when 4th Avenue in Kitsilano was the hippie counterculture mecca known as Rainbow Road—on a Friday or Saturday night after two in the morning can be a dislocating experience. At most times, the restaurant is a rustic, earnest vegetarian place for people who enjoy good, sprouty food served poorly. It is an unreconstructed, un-ironic hippie endeavour, with live folk singers strumming acoustic guitars from up on a stool and execrable New Age artwork for sale on the wall, most often photographs of ubiquitous Asian Buddha statues from someone who just got back from a trip that really changed their whole thinking on things, you know, and really opened up

their third eye. (This turn of phrase may sound like an explicit, albeit poetic, way of referring to the gastro-intestinal difficulties facing many travellers; although it isn't, I can guarantee you that if anybody starts talking to you about opening up their third eye, you will wish, *within seconds*, that it were.) Basically, the food at the Naam is delicious, iconically Vancouver, and a draw for hippies and those with patience for their vibes.

But the Naam is also one of Vancouver's only well-known, non-Chinese restaurants open twenty-four hours, and so on Friday and Saturday nights, after the shows and the clubs let out, the patchouliati are joined by the chachi nightclub crowd, and the smell of incense mingles with that of Joop! and Right Guard.

The most out-of-place Naam patrons I ever saw were two frat-house date-rapist types with whom I had to share the bathroom. As I washed my hands, the guy in the cubicle and the guy at the urinal talked shamelessly about whether the dancers at the strip club they'd just visited had made good use of the waterworks piped up through the stage; in the mirror, it was impossible to miss the reflection of urinal-guy's gigantic erection, which he had been "shaking off" for quite some time—not ten feet away, through the doors of the bathroom, it's safe to assume that somebody was discussing chakras; on opposite sides of me, the healing powers of crystal and the squealing shower of Cristal. I thought of the incident when I read, in Rex Weyler's book on the history of Greenpeace, that the "central meeting point" between the West Side progressives of Rainbow Road and the more-proletarian types from the East Side was the Cecil Hotel Pub on Granville St.[12] The romantic atmosphere he describes, where "[p]ool balls cracked and the jukebox blasted out" Aretha Franklin, Otis Redding, and the Beatles, and "draft beer were 25 cents," sounds a far sight more enticing that the seedy strip joint that the Cecil became, where a lascivious bouncer promised the nineteen-year-old me that the VIP lounge was like a "crash course in gynecology," a phrase that still turns my stomach a decade later (if you listened hard, you could still hear the sound of balls cracking).

If you talk to an older generation of leftists, the ones who spent the 1960s and '70s as hard-line Marxists rather than hippies, about the Naam, they'll inevitably tell you about a boycott campaign against the restaurant over labour issues. The Marxists' boycott always struck me as an attempt to distance themselves from what the Naam represents, distinguishing the Socialists from the cultural bohemians with whom they're conflated by the lazy political shorthand that lumps together anybody who opposes war with anybody who likes folk music. To an outsider, it may seem like the narcissism of minor differences, but to the Marxists, it's an important distinction between a revolutionary position and a solipsistic personal outburst perfectly reconcilable to the market economy at the end of the day (for what it's worth, Kits *is* where the sun goes down, too).

These kinds of criticisms would carry more weight if most of the leftists who made them didn't have cabins on Mayne Island, but the transformation of 4th Avenue specifically and Kits more

I DON'T HAVE KIDS MYSELF BECAUSE I DON'T OWN ENOUGH YOGA GEAR. THAT'S THE UNIFORM FOR MOMS IN THIS CITY—HEAD-TO-TOE LULULEMON—WHILE BUYING ORGANIC BABY FOOD—BECAUSE YOU HAVE TO HAVE A FREE-RANGE BABY—AND SPEAKING SIGN LANGUAGE TO THEIR BABIES, ALL THE WHILE PUSHING THEIR KIDS IN STROLLERS THE SIZE OF SMART CARS. HOW FAST ARE YOU RUNNING WITH A BABY THAT YOU NEED MOUNTAIN BIKE TIRES AND BRAKES? WHENEVER I SEE A HANDBRAKE ON A STROLLER, I LOSE MY MIND. WHY DO YOU NEED A HANDBRAKE? YOU GET THAT YOU'RE PUSHING IT—RIGHT? IT DOESN'T EVEN MAKE SENSE. WE ALL KNOW WHAT HAPPENS WHEN WE SLAM ON THE BRAKES. LET'S SAY YOU'RE RUNNING AROUND THE SEAWALL WITH YOUR BABY AND SOMETHING DANGEROUS HAPPENS AND YOU TRY TO STOP BY SLAMMING ON THE BRAKES—YOU'D ACTUALLY FLIP OVER THE STROLLER, AND THE LAST THING YOU WOULD SEE AS YOU WENT DOWN IS YOUR BABY, FLYING INTO THE BURRARD INLET SIGNING "HELP."

ERICA SIGURDSON

generally from hippie beacon to centre of hedonist consumption does seem to underline their case. The multicultural strip "lined with psychedelic shops and record stores" that Weyler lovingly remembers is today home to spas, upscale baby supply stores, and doggie bakeries, as well as Vancouver's indigenous, ubiquitous line of yoga clothing, lululemon, enjoyed universally by women who love comfort and men who love asses, but lamented and mocked as the ultimate symbol of yuppiness. The neighbourhood's change in tone is captured quietly in the closing lines of Bruce Serafin's profile of Stan Persky, the writer and activist and one of Kits' most famous American expats:

We looked out at the new concrete curb—so smooth and
white—that had been put in around his house since I
had last been there. It looked completely out of place,
and when I remarked on this, Persky said, "Dust. It was
dust that brought that curb. It was still a little country-
ish around here, a little dusty. Well, I liked that. But the
neighbours have nice cars and they didn't want dust on
their cars. So there you are."[13]

Perhaps my favourite piece of writing on Kits' excesses is a
Craigslist post titled "LOOKING FOR TANTRIC SEX PARTNER
- m4w - 65 (Kitsilano)." In it, a male, 65, says, "I am looking for a

woman, between 18–60, preferably single but will accept attached or married if it doesn't interfere with this, any ethnic origin, not more than a few extra pounds [...] I am looking for someone who is reasonably mature and aware of spirituality at least in a general sense, for example, has read Eckhart Tolle [...] preferable [sic] someone who does not live very far from Kitsilano [...] I will need to see a pic also."[14] Tolle is the Vancouver new-age guru known for years in Kits through his column in *Common Ground* magazine who was plucked from obscurity (and from ever having to worry about money again) by Oprah Winfrey.

Kits isn't all hippies, of course. A number of Greek immigrants chose to settle in the neighbourhood after World War II and have left their mark on the area in the form of Greek speciality food stores, annual Greek Day festivities, and the best Greek restaurants in the city.

Kits also was home to one of the most important rooms in the history of Vancouver stand-up comedy: the Urban Well, hosted by Brent Butt. For years, Brent's spot at Yew and Cornwall, right off the water, was a quality, independent stage that attracted some of the biggest talents in the city (and occasionally beyond). Although he was no longer booking it by the time I started in comedy (by then it was booked by Sean Proudlove, a brilliant stand-up who has perhaps done more than anybody else to support comedy in Vancouver), I was lucky enough to perform on the Well's ninth anniversary show, hosted by Brent and headlined by Robin Williams, who famously fell in love with the spot and would work the room whenever he was in Vancouver. For weeks after any performance by Williams, the place would be packed—a wonderful gift for the community, even if the audiences ended up being a little distracted, craning their necks during the show to see if the superstar would be making an appearance.

The stand-up scene in Vancouver still hasn't recovered from losing the Urban Well; it had been a room with a community, where comics would show up even if they weren't performing, where headliners would stop by to do a show for free. Kitsilano is a paradise lost for two of the communities I identify with most: the left and the comedy scene. So if this essay about one of the most beautiful neighbourhoods in the world seems unnecessarily acidic, you know what you can chalk it up to. At least the Greeks have never let me down.

MAIN
STREET

It certainly must speak to the confidence of and attention paid to the good-looking young people who've built the neighbourhood to meet their social and aesthetic needs that if you say Main Street in Vancouver even though the thoroughfare itself runs through the city's traditional Chinatown and Little India, residential homes and light industry, from the very northern tip of the city near the Inlet to the very southern end near the alluvial planes of Richmond and the banks of the Fraser River, one will invariably assume that you mean the twenty-two-or-so blocks between the Foundation restaurant on Seventh and the Café Montmartre on Twenty-ninth.

That strip of Main Street is one of the only neighbourhoods in Vancouver to be reinvented almost completely within a span of time that I can remember clearly at both ends. In the mid-1990s, when I was fifteen, I started hanging out at a Trotskyist bookstore called Pathfinder, near the intersection of Main and King Edward. At the time, there was a strip of ethnic mom-and-pop shops,[vii] hair salons, a bizarrely named pizza-by-the-slice place called Stasis—you're not going anywhere ... until you've tried our pizza!—and a Chinese place called the Beef Bowl. It was a generally nondescript, multiethnic working-class swath of Vancouver where you could buy several samosas for a dollar at a handful of shops (this practice, once widespread in Vancouver, seems to have largely died out). Near the intersection was the Grind, a coffee shop that, at the time, played loud industrial music and would fill up with tobacco smoke (a far cry from the quiet study hall it is today, colonized by university students), and just two doors down was Helen's Grill, a greasy spoon whose jukebox supplied the name for Vancouver author Kevin Chong's novel *Baroque-a-Nova*, but whose food I always found unappealing; across the street was a hippie Israeli falafel place called Deserts, whose counterperson was a six-foot stunner that my friends and I called "VSM," for vegan super model. Helen's and the Grind are still there, though most of the neighbourhood around them has changed drastically.

I always arbitrarily put the tipping point of Main Street's transition at Deserts being replaced with Hawker's Delight, one of the city's very best cheap restaurants (probably one of the best cheap restaurants you're going to find in *any* city), which serves incredible Malaysian and Singaporean meals for virtually nothing. Over the course of the years after Hawker's opened, the

vii. As in mom-and-pop shops owned by non-white families; not a shop where you could buy an ethnic mom and pop, like some sort of reverse Angelina Jolie thing.

neighbourhood quickly transformed into something altogether more youthful, becoming the southern, slightly more upscale half of Vancouver's hipster nerve centre, running along Main from just north of Broadway to just south of King Edward, with specialty video stores, innumerable clothing boutiques, designer furniture dealers, bike shops, and myriad other signs of aesthetic sensibility and sophisticated consumption. At the Broadway end, there's still a bit more of an East Vancouver vibe hanging in the air, with the 2400-block home to the outstanding Pulpfiction Books, the offices of Libby Davies, one of the best MPs in the country, not to mention the offices of Vancouver's comic-book super couple, Eisner-award-winning artist Pia Guerra (*Y: The Last Man*) and her also-Eisner-award-winning husband, writer Ian Boothby, also a successful improviser and comedian. While working on a piece for

Citytv about the polite society neighbours of the Fox Cinema porno theatre—which is right across the street from Davies' office—trying to get its license taken away, Boothby wrote me a note that read, "Is there a petition to sign to keep it there? It keeps our rent down." (Porn with incongruous neighbours is a theme on Main Street; at Sixteenth, a bridal-dress shop called Bello is right next to Big Rich's twenty-four-hour XXX store.)

If the denizens of Main Street are often hipsters (and they are), their sensitivity to the term is such that I once had a crowd at the recently refurbished Biltmore Cabaret turn on me simply for using it, suspecting (in this case correctly) that I meant them; the street that they've carved out for themselves seems to put paid the idea advanced in Vancouver-based *Adbusters* magazine, in the summer of 2008, that the hipster marked the dead end of Western civilization.[15]

At the time, I remember enjoying the piece, though a CBC interview with the suspiciously aloof writer led me to wonder if the whole thing hadn't been simply an exercise in meta-hipsterdom, a new assertion of exclusivity inside a once-exclusive, now flabby and accessible subculture. The piece sparked a huge, sometimes angry discussion about hipsterism and its discontents, including from Robert Dayton (a.k.a. Li'l Hamm, a.k.a. DJ Body Beautiful) on his blog We Hate Vancouver, as well as the lament "hipsters are not a crime" on the popular website Beyond Robson. One who commented on the *Adbusters* site wrote, "How bout you guys go back to the important shit, like figuring out how to transcend the market and stuff, instead of passing judgment on a bunch of twenty-somethings indulging in their youth."[16]

You'd be hard pressed to make the case that the coming of the hipsters destroyed Main Street; the fact of the matter is it's an exciting, vibrant street, with very good food and nice clothes. David Beers, editor of the online magazine the *Tyee,* once explained to me how he took his son along parts of Main, into the shops, speaking to the owners, so that the boy could see creative people finding ways to live off their creativity. Main Street will never have the easy sense of community of, say, Commercial Drive, but that has as much to do with topography as anything: Main is too steep a slope to encourage the kind of aimless strolling you can fall into on Commercial, and the street is too wide, and too busy, for Commercial's casual, back-and-forth jaywalking and across-the-street calling (if you're walking north on the east side of Commercial and see a friend walking south on the west side, you'd be obliged to stop and chat, one of you having crossed over; on Main, you'd be lucky to get a wave).

But given what they've got to work with, Main Street people have done well. Sure, there are irritating idiosyncrasies that come with the culture; for comedians, the worst, and oddest, is that hipsters have a prejudice against polished material, so that when you perform on or around Main Street you have to pretend you've just come up with everything, adding false stammers and stutters and, whenever possible, reading jokes off of a pad of paper, even if you've been telling them for years. And yes, the surliness at Our Community Bikes repair shop can be a bit much—we get it, anarcho-syndicalism places less of an emphasis on customer service—but that hardly qualifies for the end of Western civilization

(in fact, I love Our Community Bikes). But if you were to ask me whether Main Street was a nicer place to be in 1996 or today, there'd be no contest.

Of course, that's a problem, too. Everyone in Vancouver is worried about somebody gentrifying a cool place like Commercial Drive, and though that's potentially a problem, the much more pressing issue—if you're worried about gentrification—is the gentrification of *shitty* neighbourhoods. Just because Main Street in the 1990s was boring and nondescript doesn't mean that the people living and operating businesses there didn't have the right to that neighbourhood. For years, the smart money in Vancouver has been picking out spots along Kingsway and Hastings-Sunrise, finding

seams of coal that, with the right kind of pressure, could yield diamonds. In a conversation about how hideous and altogether free of
personality Kingsway is, a friend once said to me, "Yeah, but at least
it *is* the thing that it *is*." In 2008, a condo tower went up at Kingsway and Knight, and an apparently wonderful new restaurant
called Les Faux Bourgeois has gone in at Kingsway and Fraser—a
teacher friend who grew up in East Van said that he and his wife
were able to remember the specific address because of its proximity
to a legendary gang shooting from their youth. From all accounts,
the restaurant is outstanding, but it's inconceivable that anyone
would have considered opening one there five years ago.

So the issue isn't hipsterism, it's capitalism; and I call it an
"issue" because not everybody—in fact, only a minority of people—
see it as a problem. But just as freedom of expression entails the

right to say terrible things, the right for a neighbourhood to *be*, without worrying about predation from developers and real estate moguls, also means the right of shitty, boring, ugly neighbourhoods to go on being shitty, boring, and ugly. The key is working toward revitalization and creativity without tipping over into eviction and dispossession, something that Vancouver, unfortunately, is terrible at.

DAVIE VILLAGE

That the marquee event of Vancouver's West End is the annual
international fireworks competition (once called the Benson &
Hedges Symphony of Fire, then the HSBC Celebration of Light,
then the OmegaCorp Consortium of Exploding Colour-Things, or
whatever; due to the vicissitudes of corporate funding and anti-to-
bacco legislation, they're now usually referred to as "the fireworks")
is one of the great ironies of the city. Every year, Vancouver's sophisticated, beachfront, homosexual ghetto (let's call it "the gaytto")
throws itself open to hordes of the same drunken suburbanites that
every fairy living there moved to the West End to escape. It's like
if Harlem were known for its summer NASCAR race.
My dear TV co-host and stellar West End comic Erica
Sigurdson often laments onstage the paradox of gay-
bashers filling the Davie Village every summer: "This is
our neighbourhood, this is how we live. We don't go to
Surrey and read."

It's easy to see how West-End neighbourhood envy
might fit in to the typical homophobe's tendency to
resent gays. Just as they furiously suspect homos of
having a monopoly on great, guilt-free sex, the iconography of fun ("They ruined rainbows for everybody!"
"They took the word 'gay'!"), and rock-hard abs, one
might assume that they'd also be mad about the gay
claim on one of Vancouver's most magical quarters: the
majesty of English Bay—the ocean!—right up against the
lip of the city; the view of Vancouver's most beautiful
bridge (Burrard); the ability to see Kits without having
to smell the patchouli; the palm trees and the sand; the
Sylvia Hotel; the back entrance to Stanley Park (oh, stop
it!). The West End is clean, gorgeous, and well laid out; it
was *bound* to become gay.

Of course, there are shadows. White, middle-class
gayness is the cultural norm, and it seems that the price for living
in the ostensibly safe, new neighbourhood once leaving home (and
its -ophobia) is acculturation. The stereotype exists that all gays
are rich because none of them have any children and men are paid
well—in fact, a lot of hard work is put in by a lot of people who can't
actually afford to participate in the affluence of the West End, who
stay because it's all that they've got. For years, my little brother slept

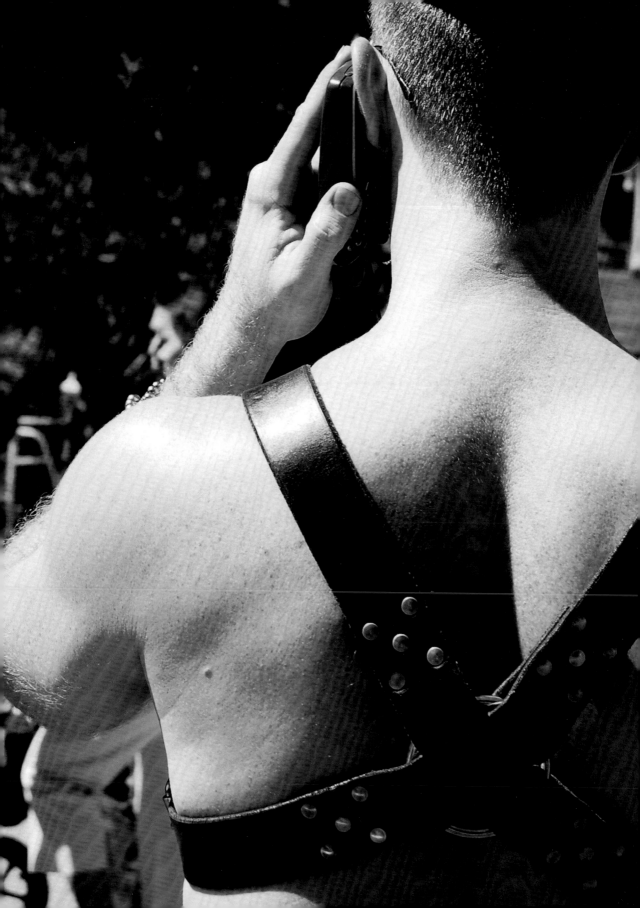

in the living room of a shared one-bedroom apartment (in a building he and his neighbours referred to colloquially as "Stack-o'-fags West," as a nod to the primary "Stack-o'-fags" building just a little to the east), working at Delany's, the gay coffee shop on Denman, though the repetitive labour was crippling his forearms with carpal tunnel and the only dental work he could afford was to have teeth pulled. Older, more comfortable men would perpetuate the fiction that they were all in the same boat, even while my brother made their drinks, expertly drawing artwork into the foam despite the pain in his hands. (None of which is meant to take away from the life-changing role of the neighbourhood in making my brother, and thousands like him, feel safe, accepted, and part of a community during some of the most important years of his life; just to say that it comes with a cost.)

The biggest shadow cast by the neighbourhood is AIDS, the tragic consciousness of which often hangs in the air. Some of the lions of the West End, the legends (artists like Joe Average and Tiko Kerr) are celebrated, but always with a bit of sadness. For many young men, the release from repression signalled by a move to the Village can be such that they briefly—sometimes permanently— lose control, with drugs and with sex, a fact of life that has broken through what ought to have been AIDS' generational quarantine. There have been great leaps in HIV treatment, slowing the illness's progression and removing some of the visible stigma associated with it. Still, under the campy fun of the neighbourhood, with its bright pink lampposts and bubble machines filling the intersection of Davie and Thurlow, there's a lot of suffering. At the heart of the community, embracing and showcasing its alternately political, sexual, campy, artistic, grieving as well as street-fighting dimensions, is Little Sister's bookstore on Davie. Between the sex accessories and the tacky homo T-shirts and the shelves of wonderful books and the staff and supporters who for decades have fought against street-level homophobia and federal government censorship and AIDS, you've got a pretty good triangulation of the soul of the neighbourhood.

One time, I bought a sex book at Little Sister's while I was there with a male friend. The cashier was helpful:

"You know, this one is actually mostly just straight stuff."

"Oh," I said, unwilling, for some reason, to tell him I was

straight. Something about it was just too *me?-I'm-not-gay* dis-
avowal, so instead I just crinkled my face up like a little girl and
said, "That's okay!" I like to imagine that that cashier thought I
was the most dedicated sodomizer in the world, so committed to
awesome gay sex that I would buy a 600-page book with only three
gay pages just to learn a couple of moves.

The West End isn't all gay, of course, nor has it always been
gay. In the 1960s—thanks to the free hand developers got from city
council[17]—apartment buildings shot up like mushrooms (there're
those phalli again); today, the residential density in the area is
among the highest in North America. And despite that, some
people still want to move the beautiful and centrally located St
Paul's Hospital.

Even if not all its residents are interior decorators, the neighbourhood's beauty makes it a natural habitat for aesthetes. It
also makes it a magnet for money, and from early on in the city's
history, folks with cash have been drawn to it. In William Harbeck's famous 1907 footage of Vancouver (the Vancouver Historical
Society released a positively breathtaking DVD of the filmmaker's
trip through what's now the Downtown Eastside, up Robson, and up
Davie), the most transporting, exotic shots are those of Davie Street
and the Gabriola Mansion, which is now the city's most stupidly
named restaurant, the Macaroni Grill (who uses a grill to make
macaroni? I mean, why not call it the Steak Kettle?). Benjamin T.
Rogers, described by Bruce Macdonald in his magisterial history
of the city as "Vancouver's first millionaire-industrialist,"[18] had the
mansion built just up from the beach, and all you can think looking
at the 1907 footage is "Yeah, of course he did. Why in the hell
wouldn't he? Why don't *I* live in the West End?"

The West End was also home to the man who is arguably, to
this day, the city's most storied black citizen, Seraphim "Joe" Fortes,
a moustachioed Barbadian immigrant who settled in the city just
two years before it became Vancouver[19]. Fortes is featured as a
character in Ethel Wilson's short story "Down at English Bay," and
he is also a pivotal minor character in Lee Henderson's novel *The
Man Game*, which won the 2009 Ethel Wilson Prize. Henderson,
though, focuses his attention on Fortes the saloon-keeper, early
into his tenure in the city, while Wilson looked, with great affec-
tion, at Fortes in his more famous role as a swimming instructor

and lifeguard (Wilson's choice was natural; she actually learned to swim from Joe Fortes).[20]

The protagonist of Wilson's short story, published in 1949, is a mildly nutty maiden aunt who earns the respect of her wary niece after calmly standing up against racial prejudice directed at a white, female friend of Joe Fortes; Aunt Topaz calmly, but with conviction, overcomes her fear of public speaking in order to vouch for both the woman as well as "our respected fellow-citizen Joe Fortes." By loving and accepting Fortes, Aunt Topaz is loved and accepted by her niece, who had otherwise been looking askance at her. It's the ultimate story of outsiders banding together and, in the end, winning the day; so too, most of the time, is the West End.

DOWNTO
EASTSID

A little while back, CBC television ran a special about the problem of drug addiction in Vancouver's tragic Downtown Eastside (DTES). It was a long piece, full of interviews that hit all the sore spots and tired plot points that Vancouverites have become used to, and weary of, in the various narratives woven together to make sense of the city's festering wound of urban blight: the outrage over pharmacists in the area enabling the addicts and profiting from their miserable habits; the interview with a sadly docile user, ashamed of his situation, sharing pathetic anecdotes about petty crime and all-encompassing enslavement to the next fix; the hard-boiled cop who has seen it all, gotten right up against the terrible scourge that the comfortable viewers at home can only dream of, seen the futility of the situation firsthand.

Though the piece was fairly well executed, I suspect that the reporter, who spoke with a thick, foreign accent, doesn't have much of a future in the world of Vancouver journalism, or many prospects for climbing the ladder. Not that I think the accent will hold him back, it's just that he's been dead for over ten years now. And besides, there aren't too many rungs left to climb when you're the doyen of Lower Mainland journalism, Jack Webster. The piece on the "East End" drug problem was filed sixty years ago and broadcast on May 13, 1959.

I came across a link to the video on one of the city's best blogs, Past Tense Vancouver ("fragments of Vancouver history and reflections thereon").[21] The blog is maintained by an activist historian with whom I went to Simon Fraser University, Lani Russwurm, who has, among other things, demolished the prevailing idea that dirty junkies and petty thieves tore a sweet little picket fence neighbourhood from the lily-white palms of functional Vancouver (what some have called the "dominant accounts [that] treat the buildings of Hastings Street as part of Vancouver's historic entitlement, 'stolen' by an urban underclass."[22] Russwurm links to a 2008 piece in the *Georgia Straight* in which then-mayoral hopeful Peter Ladner, from one of Vancouver's most distinguished, establishment families, calls for a return to the normalcy and innocence captured in a famous Fred Herzog photo called *Hastings at Columbia*, taken in 1958. Russwurm runs the photo on his blog with the following caption: "Hastings at Columbia by Fred Herzog, 1958. At the time, this intersection was the epicentre of Canada's largest drug scene."[23]

He then patiently outlines the actual history of the neighbourhood:

> The Downtown Eastside has always been the centre of
> Vancouver's hard drug trade. In fact, Canada's first drug
> prohibition law originated here, introduced a century ago
> after Mackenzie King investigated compensation claims
> stemming from the 1907 anti-Asian riots in Chinatown
> and Japantown. Some of the claims happened to come
> from opium manufacturers and King became especially
> alarmed when he learned the opium scourge was spread-
> ing to white women and girls.[24]

Russwurm goes on to explain how the "drug scene never left
this area," citing a 1955 *Maclean's* article whose title he borrows for

the blog post "The Dope Craze That's Terrorizing Vancouver," and convincingly makes the case that the situation we see today is the result of the market being driven outdoors.

The distinction between indoors and outdoors is key to how Vancouverites think about the Downtown Eastside. We often comment on how frequently the buildings are used as backdrops for American films, but we rarely mention how we who live in the city tend to think of them as façades the rest of the time, anyway. The glaring thing about the area is how everything happens outside— the sleeping, the socializing, the panhandling, the fencing—and somehow, the only way to make the phrase drug market seem more menacing is to qualify it as open air; two words that make a patio furniture set-up sound like heaven, but make the sale and consumption of drugs sound like something from out of the alternate 1985 in

Back to the Future II. Somehow, outside, the people in the Downtown Eastside are objects; inside, they can be subjects, because the indoors is where people and civilization live, which is why it can be easier to wrap one's head around the tragedy of destroying the Pantages Theatre on Hastings than the obscenity of handing out jaywalking tickets to people who can't afford breakfast in the lead-up to the Olympic Games.

One of the finest pieces of literature set in the neighbourhood, Timothy Taylor's *Story House*, centres around the rediscovery of the neighbourhood's interiors, specifically a dilapidated and mouldy piece of forgotten architecture. The crude, commercial exploitation of the rediscovery—in the novel, a reality TV show, but one that works as a metaphor for myriad planning and real estate development initiatives—ends by destroying it.

The fight for interiors is also what made the Woodward's squat of 2002, also commemorated as Woodsquat, so revolutionary and transformative an experience. All that fall, street people and activists occupied the massive, hulking Woodward's department store building (which had been vacant since 1993) and resisted the neoliberal siege that was now literal, as well as metaphorical, for nearly 100 days. The assertive beauty of the moment is fairly captured in this phone call between antipoverty activist Reverend Davin Ouimet and City Housing Manager Cameron Gray on December 12, 2002:

> Gray: Hi.
> Ouimet: Hi, Cameron.
> Gray: How are you?
> Ouimet: I'm too stubborn to die.
> Gray: [silence]
> Ouimet: I'm one of the negotiators with the Woodward's Squat and the reason why I'm phoning you is because you're the Housing Manager and I'm kind of wondering what it is you're doing to get people housing.[25]

For those of us who supported the action, it was our turn to be outside looking in, as we did during many rallies in the street outside the building. The action became iconic—the following July, as a birthday gift from a friend, I was given a print-out of artist Murray Bush's hilarious, yet somehow touching, rendering of Queen Elizabeth II's face Photoshopped over that of a squatter seated in an old chair, enjoying a smoke underneath a poster that says, "We Will Win." (The Queen had made a visit to the city that October when the squat was in full swing; Murray's poster reads, "Social Issues may not be your cup of tea but homelessness needs to be dealt with effectively. Demand provincially funded housing for the poor, disabled and elderly.")[26]

At one of the rallies for the squat, a huge ladder was propped up against the side of the building, and those who cared to see inside were invited up. Fat guys generally hate ladders, but as I negotiated it, there were familiar faces, antipoverty activists, at the top, and so I was able to persevere. Inside, the building looked like an old hangar, cavernous and filthy and unwelcoming. But the people inside were gathered in groups, large and small, some shooting the shit and making jokes, others taking votes and making decisions about the squat and its smaller, subsidiary actions. In the same way as Michael Ignatieff recalls his revulsion at the British Coal Miners' strike as the moment he realized firmly that he was a liberal and not a socialist, I remember that moment in the Woodsquat evoking precisely the opposite reaction. Unfortunately, it was a decisive event in splitting Liberals from Socialists at City Hall, too, as the newly elected progressive city council dominated by Mayor Larry Campbell and his party COPE began in-fighting over Premier Gordon Campbell's intention, quickly carried out, to send the cops in and evict the squatters.

In many ways, people in Vancouver talk about the Downtown Eastside the way that people throughout the Western world talk about Africa. Some call for apolitical charity and aid; others call for armed intervention. Everyone agrees that it's a problem to be dealt with, filled with people who are their own worst enemies and whose lives are a mess. In evaluating both Africa and the Downtown Eastside, the violence and misery that flow predictably from commercial and political decisions is chalked up to the irrationality, death drive, ignorance, and indolence of their primary victims. Just as Westerners are willing to lay the blame for the violent fallout of their desire for cell phone batteries, diamonds, and oil on atavistic, dark-continent tribalism, law enforcement and real estate developers and city planners are willing to credit the least powerful people in the city with somehow presenting its biggest obstacle:

That which now characterizes the neighbourhood open drug markets, the deepening poverty and desperation, the run-down streetscape are products of the same forces which induced the proliferation of condo towers, art galleries, restaurants, cafés, nightclubs, townhouses, heritage neighbourhoods, and inner city middle class consumers. Zones of darkness and despair and zones of happy prosperity are parts of the same city. The open drug market along Hastings Street appeared at precisely the same time that condos were being built around Gastown.[27]

One way of thinking about the DTES as analogous to Africa that is rarely mentioned, but might be the most empowering, is as the cradle and fount of civilization, the knowing that, somewhere back along the line, we all come from there. The community struck up around the Hastings Mill and "Gassy Jack" Deighton's saloon—an area first called Gastown, then Granville, before its final christening in 1886—is the nucleus of this city's history. Vancouver storytellers looking for a hard, narrative kernel indigenous to the city have worked its oldest neighbourhood to great and gritty effect in novels like Taylor's *Story House* or George Fetherling's *Jericho*. In the DVD *City Reflections,* in which Vancouver historians narrate the oldest filmed footage of Vancouver, a voiceover explains why a streetcar has to turn slightly, as trolley buses still do today more than a century later, as it crosses Cambie on Hastings, entering the "worst block in Vancouver." As discussed by Jeff Sommers and Nick Blomley in *Every Building on 100 West Hastings*: this spot is where the grid of the original city, Granville/Gastown, meets up with the new one, the rest of Vancouver. It's worth remembering that it wasn't Gastown that changed, introducing an aberration into the grid—it was the city around it. And yet I can be almost certain that most people would be inclined to blame the slightly awkward shift on the Downtown Eastside. Somehow, it *must* be their fault.

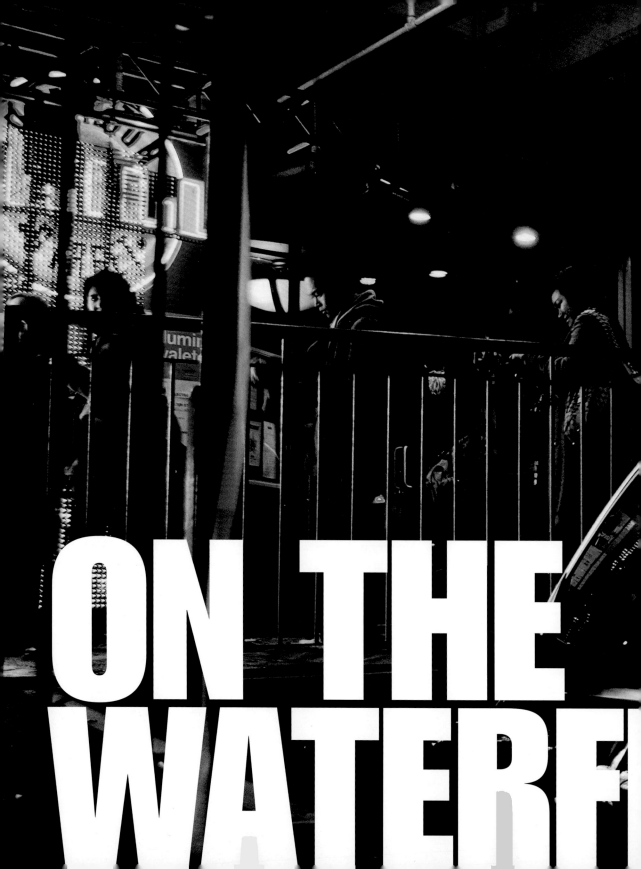

ON THE
WATERF

Each on its own shore of False Creek, Yaletown and Granville Island/False Creek South are like half-siblings born of very, very different fathers. Yaletown is the neo-liberal echo to Granville Island's Trudeau-era, government-interventionist project. Separated by a generation, with one mostly leading into Expo 86 and the other mostly leading out of it, each development reclaimed a piece of Vancouver's False Creek waterfront industrialism, spinning it into shops, residences, and community spaces. The two points are connected by the city's jaw-dropping seawall, as well as by competing lines of mini-ferries darting back and forth across the water. They are separated, obviously, by False Creek and (just as obviously, if you're looking) by completely different philosophies about building cities and communities.

For some, saying that a neighbourhood will be "the new Yaletown" is their way of pronouncing a once-cool area dead, balefully predicting that it will soon be beyond their own economic reach, the reach of the community already living there, as well as the reaches of the kinds of people they want to hang out with. In their critical essay "The Worst Block in Vancouver," Jeff Sommers and Nick Blomley point out how affluent Vancouver thinks of the Downtown Eastside as a contagion posing a threat to the healthy parts of the city, without ever considering how the rest of the city's economic behaviour affects the DTES.[28] Yaletown is the obverse of that prejudice; in the eyes of no-money Vancouver, *it's* the neighbourhood that threatens to spill over, taking the rest of the city down with its culture of addiction to destructive uppers, like wheat grass and condo-flipping.

But the sentence "That neighbourhood is going to be the new Yaletown" is one of those rare Vancouver phrases—like "Immigration has transformed this city" or "The Olympics are going to change everything"—whose words can be spoken in the same order by people who mean to express diametrically opposed levels of enthusiasm. It's also easy to imagine the words "the new Yaletown" breathlessly leaving the lips of an ecstatic developer or a real estate agent with an erection. At least one suburban project a few years back, called Quattro, went with the marketing tagline "Yaletown Comes to Surrey," which doesn't sound like it'd be fun for either community—unless it were only the first half of the headline "Yaletown Comes to Surrey, Gets Ass Kicked." In 2007, a sly Flickr photographer called mylosh snapped a photo of one of Quattro's SkyTrain station poster ads, which showed the importance of good neighbours. The transit advertising company, Lamar, mounts its ads in pairs, and next to Quattro's attempt to turn the Fraser Highway into the *Frasier* Highway, was an anti-car-theft propaganda poster with three angry cops in an underground parking garage, holding back a snarling police dog; "Yaletown Comes to Surrey," then "We're Closing in on Car Thieves."[29]

Yaletown is developer Concord Pacific's free-market Vancouverism unleashed, born from the fire sale of the Expo lands and subject to nothing like the rigorous, constructive strictures placed on Granville Island/False Creek South by various levels of government. The authors of *City Making in Paradise* seem unduly happy with how Yaletown turned out, though that may have something to do with their being impressed at the hurdles it's overcome (namely, in their eyes, Pacific Boulevard and BC Place).[30] They praise the way it "knits the old warehouse district with the new high-rise brick fascia construction," seemingly unperturbed by the fact that, though it may knit building designs together, its social exclusion breaks people apart. The same authors point out that "False Creek South's most important characteristic was the diversity of its residents,"[31] and if that's the case, then certainly Yaletown's socio-economic monoculture can't be a good thing.

Besides the odd event at the beautiful Roundhouse Community Centre, Yaletown is a civically uninteresting and uninterested place. In Kits, on Commercial, Main Street, Granville Island, Cambie, and even Robson, both yuppies and bus-transfer types can find something of interest—for all the yoga stores and spas and doggy bakeries on 4th Avenue, there's also Duthie Books and a Does Your Mother Know? magazine store and a Zulu Records; on the Drive, for all the People's Co-Op left-wing bookstores and vegan food outlets and djembe-drum-circle assemblies there's upscale Lime sushi and Dream Designs furniture and accessories and stores selling fine art. Those mixes make for great neighbourhoods, even if (in the Vancouver tradition) they aren't neighbourhoods per se, but long, single-street strips of shops surrounded by residences.

Which adds yet another dimension to the tragedy of Yaletown: it's one of the great spaces in Vancouver—one of the few spots for a New York- or Toronto-style quarter with several blocks of *city* life in every direction. And what do we do? We blow it all on stores devoted to fancy haircuts, European furniture, and $90 T-shirts.

The neighbourhood's counterpart across the water is, by contrast, a clinic in mixed-use. Some people don't like Granville Island. In his essay "No Recipe for Funk" in the *Vancouver Review*, author and activist Matt Hearn, one of the pioneers of the city's Car-Free Day festivals, expressed an uneasiness about the island's vaguely inorganic quality and middle-class character.[32] While I'll grant Hearn that GI lacks the grounded authenticity of well-established neighbourhoods like the Drive or Strathcona or even Kits, and that there's definitely something grating about the pan-flute busking and Vancouver kitsch on offer for tourists, I can say—having worked on Granville Island and performed there countless times—that it is certainly the site of an organic community, as well as subset communities of artists, vendors, artisans, farmers, buskers, and regular customers. Hearn gets no argument from me that the dominant aesthetic is middle-class, but False Creek South, the residential area adjacent to Granville Island, was built with the now famous (and now usually abandoned) one-third, one-third, one-third formula that divided the housing market—enough for tens of thousands of people—among top-end market places, social housing, and modest, mid-level housing.[33] After a party in the courtyard of a co-op at the entrance to Granville Island, the hostess described to me the decades that she had lived in the building, sometimes on assistance, sometimes on a teacher's salary, always as a single mother.

The residential mix of False Creek South is mirrored in the mixed usage of the commercial space on the island: theatres, restaurants, the Emily Carr University of Art + Design, the Public Market, and the kids-only toy mall (whose outsize, hanging Pinocchio marionette terrified me when I was little; I was convinced that it would fall and crush the people underneath it, and was surprised to find out as an adult that it's about five feet tall). Cultural tumult on Granville Island is omnipresent: the Vancouver Fringe Festival takes over the island and its myriad stages every fall, followed quickly by the Vancouver International Writers' Festival; the Comedy Festival was held there during its formative years; and there are sculptors and glass-blowers and improv comics and theatre types working and milling there constantly. My last job before we started *The CityNews List* was working at the Granville Island Tea

Company, where the staff members know as much about tea as any sommelier knows about wine. Working on Granville Island was one of the only experiences I've had where working somewhere I loved as a kid didn't ruin it, but made it better (don't even *talk* to me about my summer sweeping up fries and compacting garbage at the PNE).

Cross the water again, and the city's newest neighbourhood, South East False Creek, is just taking shape. It's the first time in Vancouver's history that adding the word "East" to a phrase actually made it swankier. Over the course of the area's development, which includes the athlete's village for the Olympic Games, the city abandoned the one-third, one-third, one-third model that made Granville Island such a success story. Instead, it planned on units selling for whatever the market would bear, along with a few spaces for social housing (in other words, market-will-bear droppings). Just the other day, a friend said to me, "That neighbourhood is going to be the new Yaletown." I think I know which way she meant it.

93

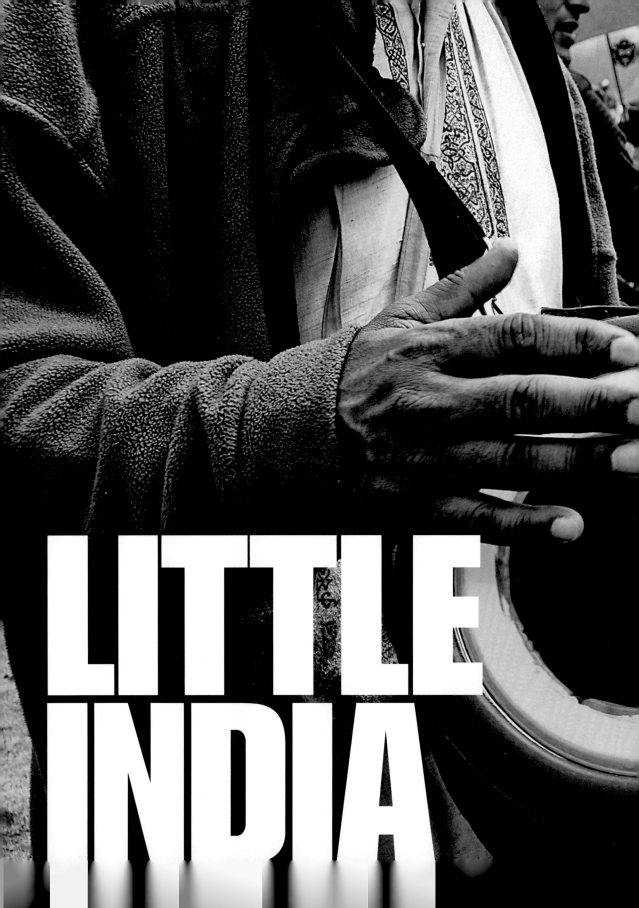

In my early twenties, I acted as the white mascot for the Main Kabob Hut on 49th Avenue in Little India (though, as some of my friends pointed out, the grammar of the name suggested "main" as in the *primary* kabob hut of all the world's sundry kabob huts, it was actually "Main" as in street). I was living just across the road, in my first place after leaving home, overlooking the intersection that had for decades been the hub of Vancouver's Punjabi community.

The scene at the Kabob Hut was as if British writer Hanif Kureishi had written an adaptation of *Cheers*, the centre of which was Ali, a tall, middle-aged, moustachioed Indo-Fijian with a high voice that sounded tiny in his mouth. He seemed to be known as Sammy by roughly an equal number of people as knew him as Ali. His business partner was a short, jovial Pakistani with an absurdly thick head of hair combed game-show style—I think he was called Nazir, but I have trouble remembering because he sold his shares to Ali/Sammy early into my stay in the neighbourhood. Finally, there was Tariq, a supremely handsome Afghani amateur boxer whose domain was the *tandoor* over which he stood all day gently palming spiced ground beef into tubes along long metal rods before plunging them into the hot, round clay oven in what was the most insanely sexual non-sexual act I've ever seen.

I was a daily fixture in the Kabob Hut, occasionally paying like any other customer, but most often being fed in exchange for a series of chores and services classified collectively under the heading "*gora* delivery" (*gora* is the rough, South-Asian equivalent of *gringo*): sometimes there'd be a delivery two blocks away to one of the *panwallas* selling Bollywood magazines alongside the sweet betel-leaf treats, so I'd take it over and get a beef-stuffed *keema naan* for my efforts; sometimes Ali needed a few jugs of milk and would send me over to the Persian market, and I would bring him back his milk and his change, and he would give me a plate of the new chili chicken he was thinking of introducing. I tried working behind the counter once, but that was a little too much, especially for my Indian friends from outside the neighbourhood who reacted the way you might if you ordered wonton soup somewhere in Chinatown and the waiter who brought it turned out to be your old friend Vinny, wearing his track suit and a heavy medallion. Mostly, I just helped out with whatever kinetic business plan *du jour* Ali came up with, and there were many—Ali suffered from some sort of entrepreneurial version of attention deficit disorder, leaping from new coats of paint to Western-style fried chicken under heat lamps as the secrets to saving his business; in fact, he probably would have done okay had he just cleaned up the bathroom and developed an even passing familiarity with FOODSAFE.

Ali routinely referred to me as his son, and to himself as my second father (he was introduced as such to my real dad whenever he visited); he even talked about taking me back to Fiji on a trip, to go scuba diving and arrange a marriage to a nice Fijian girl for me (my first impulsive, beauty-provoked kiss at age four or five had been stolen from one of the Prasad girls from two houses over, so maybe he was on to something). I loved sitting around bullshitting with Tariq, eating with our hands; he was great at shit-shooting, though every once in a while there would be a macabre reminder of the wars ravaging his homeland when he would casually drop an anecdote about a friend he had buried. We would all sit and chat, eating, while I exaggerated my *Québecosité* in order to seem more ethnic and to get in on complaining about the British Empire, which often worked: one time at Kabob Hut I was approached by an Iraqi who had been attracted by a pro-Palestinian button on my bag, and he asked me what my background was. When I told him, he deadpanned, "Ah, so you *also* have terrorism in your blood."

Main Kabob Hut was the underdog restaurant of the intersection. Most popular among tourists to the neighbourhood was the mostly crummy All-India Sweets, full of hippies and Langara students playing Russian roulette with their anuses. Just down the block from All-India was the far superior Himalaya, owned by Little India's *seigneur*, a short, massive, powerful man named Pabla. Himalaya's menu is virtually identical to All-India's, only good (but don't eat from the buffet at either). Himalaya even has an old, white waiter who has been there forever, some kind of more-permanent *gora* delivery service.

Contrary to popular belief, the food in Little India is generally not top drawer; when I lived there, Kabob Hut and Himalaya were the only good restaurants. All-India was essentially bad, though it was like eating at the high-end Vij's compared to the execrable Ismaili restaurant now mercifully gone from its spot on the east side of the street. A friend and I once made the mistake of poking our heads in, and the owner desperately pursued us out onto the sidewalk, insisting that we try his food. The restaurant's interior was a bizarre, woody, almost Old West structure, the walls plastered with patently forged celebrity autographs endorsing the food (Burt Reynolds, for instance, was a huge, *huge* fan) along with photos of the owner with no hair on the top of his head, which really undermined the effect of the wig he was wearing at the time.

Little India is officially known as the Punjabi Market, though the neighbourhood is actually a multicultural effort. Many ethnically Gujarati Ismailis from Africa live on the blocks spoking out from the Main and 49th intersection, as well as Persian (both Muslim and Baha'i) and Filipino shopkeepers, whose SkyFlakes, pork rinds, and Adobo-flavoured cracker nuts I ate just as often as I ate anything curried. The Persians' ninety-nine-cent pita bread was also a staple, as were, unfortunately, the pizza subs from the Esso station, which was the only place open after eight or nine (like Chinatown, the other ethnic-satellite neighbourhood at the other end of the city, Little India is a ghost town as of the late evening, which is its worst feature next to its physical isolation from any other cool neighbourhood).

The joy I got from the first few months of living in Little India was unabashedly Orientalist. The sound of Indian music rattling through tinny outdoor speakers bent both geography and time, and the smell of curry and clay oven cooking was constant. For the first month or so, every time I stepped out onto the street it felt like I was living overseas: the sidewalks were so *lively*, the bilingual street signs in English and Punjabi were so *cool*.

But fairly quickly, the neighbourhood just became home. As residents, we definitely possessed the social space that so many people seem to want, the easy mix of commercial transaction and casual friendship with the people who live nearby. The energy of the neighbourhood was such that it was chosen—after a gruelling, Canada-wide search—to be the setting of what was supposed to be CBC's new afternoon flagship show, a *Coronation Street*-style ensemble drama. Unfortunately, *49th & Main* wasn't particularly good (the first mistake was inversing the name of our intersection) and lasted only six episodes. But in the lead-up, at least, Little India was excited.

Not that things were always peaceable. For a period of a few weeks, nearly every night one or the other of the barbershops across from each other on 49th—one on the ground floor of my building,

the other next to the Kabob Hut—had its windows broken in a series of retaliatory smashings (even before the war, many visitors to my place were bemused to find that despite having moved to the neighbourhood of a group generally known for not cutting its hair, I was surrounded by barbers; it was like I was in a Jewish tenement block filled with pork butchers and shellfish mongers and movie haters). But even if the barbershop rivals didn't get along with each other, the residents all got along with them. The barber who worked in my building was tall and bespectacled, with his large head shaved down to the skin; to be honest, he looked as though a mad scientist had gotten into that transporter from *The Fly* with Nusrat Fateh Ali

Khan. When I moved, he bought some of my exercise equipment, gleefully sharing his Maoist philosophy with me when he saw the leftist books I was also selling; his grinning insistence that power flowed from the barrel of a gun seemed to stand in stark contrast to the federal Liberal signs placed prominently around his shop at election time. As for the ashy, elfin barber across the street, he found me once at the counter of the Kabob Hut, and invited me back to his shop for drinks. I sat there drinking Crown Royal highball after Crown Royal high-

ball, smelling the various hair-treatment products and looking at the blue divider curtains while the barber and his friend conversed in Punjabi. The only English he spoke was when he insisted, time after time, on refilling my glass, against my protestations. Later on I stumbled back home and threw up.

One of my very closest friends, Tejpal, who at that time lived in New Westminster, loved that he had a Little India homebase in my apartment. The view of the Vaisakhi parade from my balcony was uninterrupted, as was, unfortunately, the sound from the interminable speeches of politicians who flocked to Main Street's Vaisakhi in order to avoid the controversy that often surrounded the much larger Surrey celebration, known for its occasional outbursts of Sikh fundamentalism; the orange turbans of the Khalistani (Sikh separatist) movement are apparently far more common out there.

As much as he loved visiting, Tejji would lament that I'd never seen the intersection in its heyday, before Surrey, when Main and 49th really was the only game in town and even the alleyways were teeming with life. Today, Little India has lost its primacy to Surrey, in much the same way Chinatown has lost out to Richmond. In both cases, earlier-settled, working-class communities have been usurped by more recently arrived middle classes, once eager to drive in to the old neighbourhood but now happy to have the foods, clothing, and entertainments of the old country brought to them in the suburbs. The Main Kabob Hut has long since been sold by Ali/Sammy, and Tariq is now boxing for money. But Main and 49th is still the best place to get Indian fabric in the city proper, Himalaya still has a killer *aloo parantha*, and you can still get your hair cut almost anywhere.

SUBURB

Right up into the late 1920s, Vancouver was eating suburbs like a little Prussia; the "Greater Vancouver movement," as historian Daniel Francis calls it, took in the Hastings Townsite and District Lot 301, a massive land mass to the east and a smaller one to the south, respectively, in 1910. Over the next twenty years, Vancouver would also assimilate the cities of Point Grey and South Vancouver.[34] The metropolitan beast was sated until the late 1960s, when Vancouver cast a curious eye east to Burnaby, just over Boundary Road.[35]

Burnaby, the city where I grew up (which was named for one of the crooked white guys who worked with Colonel Moody to turn rampant land speculation into personal wealth), is in some ways, as a friend calls it, "an extension of East Van." For the most part, what you get on one side of Boundary Road is what you get on the other: northeast Vancouver has a lot of Chinese and Italians, so does North Burnaby; southeast Vancouver has modest, working-class homes sprinkled with large, extended- and multi-family South and East Asian houses, and so does the South Slope of Burnaby. The one bit of disconnect is the middle part of the frontier, from Moscrop to Kingsway, which goes from working class on the Vancouver side to distinctly petit bourgeois on the other. Growing up in Burnaby, we told people from out of town that we were from Vancouver, and as soon as we were old enough, we spent all of our time in the city.

But Burnaby has its own history and identity, too—as a multi-ethnic, social democrat-voting city built around Metrotown Mall. To give you an idea of the pace at which it's growing, the elementary school that I attended, Marlborough, had around 200 students when I started there in 1984, and rented out several of its classrooms to various high school re-entry programs, along with an entire second building to an English-as-a-second-language school called Columbia College. By September 2007, the school had over 1,000 students and was using both buildings. The area is now home to a large population of immigrants and refugees from the former Yugoslavia, the first of whom were arriving when I was a student.

More recently, the idea of mega-city amalgamation—joining Vancouver and the rest of the Greater Vancouver Regional District (GVRD), to form Metro Vancouver (twenty-one municipalities with a population just over two million) in the style of Toronto or Montréal has been brought forward by political scientist Kennedy Stewart, writing in *Vancouver* magazine in April 2005. Although his

idea for the mega-city didn't stick, his suggestion of a regional police force has become a serious part of the law-enforcement debate. Stewart's image of a car thief letting out a triumphant, cowboy shriek as he passes over Boundary Road is just barely an exaggeration, and many worry that as the Lower Mainland faces gang wars and organized crime networks with international connections, police are stuck in silos separating Vancouver from its neighbours; although, on the plus side, it's harder to Taser someone from inside a silo. But further integration of anything beyond law enforcement seems unlikely at this point in time. Each of the municipalities in the GVRD, like Burnaby, has its own distinct style and reputation (with the exception, I imagine, of Electoral District A, which seems to be some sort of bizarre backyard to the North Shore).

Richmond and Surrey are the two most racialized suburbs, indelibly associated in the public mind with the Chinese and Punjabi communities respectively (though Koreans are increasingly becoming associated with Coquitlam, and the resemblance between the North Shore mountains and the Zagros in Iran is supposedly the reason so many Persians settled in West Vancouver).[viii] Many people love to tell stories about how the Hong Kong Chinese left the city-state in its last days as a British colony for Richmond because its name suggested vast fortunes to come. Although I'm sure this may have been true in some cases—and it's certainly attested to by the fact that Toronto's Richmond Hill is also heavily populated by affluent Chinese, apparently for the same reason—I'm inclined to believe that a great many more people moved there because that's where the rest of the Hong Kong Chinese were going. Today, Richmond has Chinese food so good that my Hong Kongese parents-in-law don't come straight over to our house when they land at the Vancouver airport, but instead head directly to a favourite Richmond noodle house.

Surrey is the cultural whipping boy of the GVRD; it's Vancouver's New Jersey, except that New Jersey gave the world Philip Roth and Bruce Springsteen. Surrey is a city seemingly without zoning, and so makes no sense as you drive through it (which you essentially have to do, even though the SkyTrain line cuts deeply into the city—fitting, because people in the city get cut deeply next to the SkyTrain).

Across the Burrard Inlet from Vancouver are two cities connected to downtown by the Guinness family's Lions Gate Bridge: North Vancouver and West Vancouver (even though I was born and bred here, it's still confusing for me to straighten out the fact that somehow West Vancouver, the West Side, and the West End were not only different places, but nowhere near each other).[ix] North Vancouver is a charming little city with great shops and wonderful restaurants (there's a German restaurant next to the Lonsdale Quay that actually has a picture of Kaiser Wilhelm on the wall) and is, apparently, the safest place in the Lower Mainland. West Vancouver has a lot of money and no time to talk to you.

Two of Vancouver's suburbs looked initially as though they would forever be bigger, more important urban centres than the upstart between False Creek and the Inlet. Port Moody is the Jennifer Aniston to the CPR's Brad Pitt—originally set to be Terminal

viii. The wealthier ones, at least, especially those who left immediately after the revolution in 1979; many of the leftists who arrived once Khomeini tightened his grip in 1983 ended up in East Van, Burnaby, and other suburbs.

ix. The West Side is the part of Vancouver west of Main Street, south of False Creek; West Vancouver is an affluent city on the North Shore of the Burrard Inlet; the West End is on the Downtown peninsula, north of Burrard and west of Robson. Culturally, they signify Rich, Rich, and Gay, respectively.

City, Port Moody was passed over at the last minute for Vancouver, a fact that it tried catatonically to deny for years by naming every landmark and cultural event in the city after the Golden Spike, meant to be the last one hammered into the railroad. Today, Port Moody has become a great town, blessed with incredible mountain and waterway scenery even closer than Vancouver's. The centrepiece of the new Port Moody, Newport Village (designed on the Whistler Village model) overcame a serious public relations problem when two high-profile gangsters, the Red Scorpions' Dennis Karbovanec and Jonathan Bacon (of the infamous Bacon Brothers), were finally arrested there. The two had been living in a Newport Village condo building that had seen a corresponding exodus from neighbours trying to avoid gang-war crossfire; the mayor of Port Moody even weighed in to let them know that they weren't welcome.

The Fraser River waterfront of the Lower Mainland's other once-great city, New Westminster, has fallen into disrepair. Huge swaths of New West are fine, idyllic neighbourhoods full of heritage homes, and yet, performing stand-up comedy at the Lafflines Club at Columbia Station has the distinctly rough-edged feel of a road gig, even if it's a fifteen-minute train ride from my house. Historic waterfront buildings that ought to be preserved as part of the region's history have gone feral, with raccoons visible in the windows from the street. When I was a kid, the bike ride from our place on the Burnaby South Slope to the New Westminster Quay was a highlight; today there's not much there to get excited about.

There are a ton of little cities and villages around the Lower Mainland that sometimes feel very much a part of Vancouver (like during a Canucks playoff run) and sometimes feel very much apart from Vancouver (like during an election, or a conversation about whether same-sex-themed children's books have any place in schools), and the appeals of amalgamation are unlikely to transcend the narcissism of small differences and big budgets. But Vancouver's famous real estate prices don't just push up; they push out, too, and the suburbs will increasingly be peopled by expat Vancouverites. A mega-city might be the only way they can afford to get the V-word back into their addresses.

FIRST
NATIONS

In an iconic scene in Arthur Penn's 1970 film *Little Big Man*, the Cheyenne elder Old Lodge Skins, played by the charismatic Tsleil-Waututh Coast Salish writer-performer Chief Dan George (born Geswanouth Slahoot on the North Shore of the Burrard Inlet in the last year of the nineteenth century), takes his adoptive grandson, played by Dustin Hoffman, up onto a hilltop to watch him challenge Death to a fight. "It is a good day to die," Old Lodge Skins says, sparring with oblivion before lying down on the dry ground and shutting his eyes, closing his face into a death mask. The stillness of his face is only broken when his muscles begin to twitch in response to a new rain. Opening his eyes, disoriented, he asks his grandson, "Am I still in this world?" When he's answered in the affirmative, he exhales a *hey* (the tonality seems borrowed from Hoffman's people; it sounds more like an *oy* than anything else) and then says, "I was afraid of that."

The rain isn't at all like the famous rain that falls on Vancouver—it comes out of nowhere and in a torrent, whereas ours hangs in the air at first (if it hasn't rained in a while, you can smell the mossiness of it for twenty minutes before it comes) before falling more gently, and forever. But the existential question—*Am I still in this world?*—the trepidation on the borderland between one time, one reality, and another, seems appropriate to Chief Dan George's part of the world and the times when he lived in it. Many of those who authored the city of Vancouver and the projects that brought it about sought to stamp out the civilizations of George's ancestors and kin; many of the city's postcolonial critics indict it for having succeeded in that endeavour. And yet for all that dislocation and dispossession and disease, the fallout from a new society imposed on the Musqueam (mostly in what are now South Vancouver, Point Grey, and the University Endowment lands), Squamish (mostly near False Creek and the Burrard Inlet) and Tsleil-Waututh (on the North Shore), George and others still manage to be an integral part of it.

"During the 1920s," writes Bruce Macdonald in a note on the actor, "George was a Vancouver longshoreman, working on the shores of the Burrard Inlet as had his ancestors for generations."[36] Vancouver author and historian Rolf Knight situates Dan George in the broader world of the city's multi-ethnic resource-extraction and port-city proletariat—a working class that, contrary to popular perceptions and intuitions, included a diverse range of aboriginal

workers, both indigenous to the city and from elsewhere in the province. In fact, in 1906, "Indian dock workers had established the first union organization on the Burrard docks,"[37] Local 526 of the anarcho-syndicalist Industrial Workers of the World. After going through the residential school system (where he was christened with the name that most people know him by), "[f]or much of his adult working life Dan George was a longshoreman in the world that has been outlined here ... Some time later, [he] organized a musical band which performed assorted cabarets, where he delivered pungent humour in straight-faced puns."[38] Today, George's family is still a part of the city: one of his granddaughters is the author Lee Maracle; another, Charlene Aleck, was on *The Beachcombers*; his great-granddaughter, Columpa Bobb, is a multi-disciplinary artist.

Stories like George's and his family's sharpen the paradox of Vancouver as an infant city in a physical geography that has been inhabited without interruption, by complex societies, for millennia. Optimistic denialists—like those packaging an aboriginal aesthetic for tourists at the 2010 Olympics—would celebrate Vancouver as simply the friendly, sometimes bumpy introduction of Europeans and Asians into a fun Salish town. More critically, others might see the city as the colonial nightmare spun out from the void of destroyed societies, written in blood on a tabula rasa. In his play *The Damnation of Vancouver*, poet Earle Birney puts these bleak, haunting words into the mouth of a Salish chief:

> The strangers choked my son with a rope.
> From that day there was no growing in my nation.
> I had a daughter. She died young, and barren
> From the secret rot of a sailor's thighs.
> When the measles passed from our village
> There were ninety to lift into the burial grove.
> But the loggers had felled our trees,
> There was only the cold earth, and nine men left to dig.
> The doctor set fire to the longhouses and the carvings.
> My cousins paddled me over the Sound
> To sit alone by their smokehouse fire, for I, their Chief, was blind.
> One night I felt with shuffling feet the beach-trail.
> I walked into the saltwater,
> I walked down to the home of the Seal Brother...
>
> Peace to my cousins, comfort and peace.[39]

Although it's easy to sympathize with, and be incredibly moved by, the socialist Birney's lament for a lost civilization (not to mention his commendable, unfashionable early interest in this theme), the victims in his verse turn out to be far more resilient in real life. The story of Dan George and his family is part of the history of both the Coast Salish societies who have been here for millennia as well as the settler society built over the course of the last 100 years and change.

A microcosm of this relationship can be found along the roads of Stanley Park, which were initially paved with the midden left by its original inhabitants—the brand new project of a nascent city was *literally* paved with the archaeological record of the society that preceded it. When historian Jean Barman chose to document the darker history of Stanley Park and the stories of its expelled inhabitants (stories collected, often, from the descendants of those who'd been removed) in her book *Stanley Park's Secret*, she picked a potent symbolic story to unravel. Captain Vancouver first encountered the Squamish near the First Narrows of the Burrard Inlet, close to where the park is today. Many non-indigenous Vancouverites had their first encounters with First Nations iconography in the park, through its world-famous totem poles or, after 1984, Bill Reid's bronze killer whale statue outside the Aquarium, "Chief of the Undersea World"; these works infused the "natural" universe of the park with a vague Indian-ness, in the best cases leading to an understanding of Native ownership, and in the worst cases reducing Natives to landscape. After Barman's work, it's impossible to think of the park as natural, having been manicured just as much socially as horticulturally—"[i]t was not even first-growth forest," she explains.[40]

As well as those of the Coast Salish who had been living in the park, Barman explores the lives of the first wave of settlers who sought to enjoy their new home on the terms of the people whose home it had already been. I'm particularly drawn to the story of Portuguese Joe Silvey, from the island possession of Açores, because for two summers I worked as a landscaper with an old, Archie Bunker-type Portuguese guy also named Joe, also from Açores. My Joe commuted to our worksite in Port Moody—along the Barnet Highway, just off the Burrard Inlet—from my old neighbourhood on the South Slope in Burnaby; he insists that he yelled at me when I was a kid for riding my bike on his grass. True to his political style, this Joe was no particular partisan of Native rights: he would tell stories of the time he fought an Indian who mocked his English in his early years in the province, working for the railways, and I would often spend my lunch breaks cringing at his prejudice. For his part, the original Portuguese Joe, Joe Silvey, married a part-Musqueum, part-Squamish woman named Khaltinaht in a traditional Native ceremony.[41] According to Bruce Macdonald, it "was the first marriage of a non-Native to a Native in what later became Vancouver, and their first child, Elizabeth Silvey, was the first person born of a non-Native parent" in what would become the city.[42]

Vancouver is also home to many indigenous persons from other parts of the province and the country. Although Rolf Knight outlines the stories of myriad labourers making the trek into Vancouver for work, the city's first *celebrity* aboriginal-from-elsewhere was the Anglo-Mohawk writer and performer E. Pauline Johnson (Tekahionwake). Despite coming from the Six Nations reserve in Ontario, she became involved with the Squamish people after meeting Chief Joe Capilano in 1906 when Capilano and other leaders were in London, England, trying unsuccessfully to get an audience with the King to address the worsening situations facing Vancouver's original inhabitants.[43] A few years later, Johnson moved to Terminal City, where she spent the rest of her life and spun a wonderful book of ersatz-Squamish myths out of her conversations with the chief in English as well as Chinook, a hybridized language of indigenous and non-indigenous vocabulary and syntax, used widely in pioneer Vancouver and often appearing untranslated in Johnson's book, *Legends of Vancouver.*[44] (Today, the commemoration of Chinook language has become a sort of left-wing pet project in BC. A Facebook group dedicated to Chinook jargon has, as of this writing, 114 members; I'm sure you can send a *tillicum* request to any one of the administrators.)

Most of the First Nations people who've migrated to Vancouver haven't shared Johnson's experience of the city—she was celebrated and embraced by both Natives and non-Natives, becoming part of the fabric of the young town—while many others arriving since have found the city less welcoming by far. When in 1998 Vancouver police officers left Frank Paul, a Mi'kmaq originally from the Maritimes, drunk in an alley outside in the cold, where he died of hypothermia, the news short-circuited the self-congratulating mindset of many Vancouverites: that's the kind of shit that redneck cops do out in the Prairies, not in a civilized mosaic like Vancouver. But, in fact, Vancouver has no right to look down its nose at anyone; our city's racist indifference to the steady disappearance of dozens of mostly aboriginal women into the gears of a killing machine in Port Coquitlam, likely the country's most prolific serial murderer, is a shame unparalleled by that of any other city in Canada—a country with a coast-to-coast history of precisely this sort of racism.

Vancouver's saddest story is one that you hear often: a poor, young Native, or Native family, leaving the frying pan on the reserve for the fire of the city. Haisla author Eden Robinson's chilling short story "Traplines" begins with a "limp," "dead" marten being fished out from a trap—it's "the best time for trapping" because they're "hungry"—before we follow a reservation teenager, Will, bounce between a devastated and violent family and an eerily perfect, childless "townie" couple, the Smythes, who want to take him in. Rejecting both options, Will and a friend decided to leave for the big city. The story concludes:

> We catch a ride home. Billy yabbers about Christmas in Vancouver, and how great it's going to be, the two of us, no one to boss us around, no one to bother us, going anywhere we want. I turn away from him. Watch the trees blur past. I guess anything'll be better than sitting around, listening to Tony and Craig gripe.[45]

As the Vancouver reader finishes the story, it becomes clear that, all along, Vancouver is the trap to avoid.

Slightly more optimistic—or at least mixed in her assessment—is Dan George's granddaughter Lee Maracle in her short story "Polka Partners, Uptown Indians and White Folks," which opens: "When I was a petulant youth, it never ceased to amaze me how we could turn the largest cities into small towns. Wherever we went we seemed to take the country with us. Downtown—the skids for white folks—was for us just another village, not really part of Vancouver."[46]

Some might be offended by the characterization of the hapless, snotty, or oblivious white folks in Maracle's opening, but I resign myself to it. There has been no greater satire of white liberal (or, in this case, white radical) guilt-paranoia than my prepping to write this essay. What if I spelled something wrong, marking me as a racist? What if I failed to outline the intricacies of the Musqueam land claims against the University Endowment Lands and their relationship to the city? If the people can't count on a 2,500-word essay by a white stand-up comedian to sum up thousands of years of Coast Salish history and centuries of European colonial-settlerism, then what can they count on?

In my nervousness about getting it wrong, I reminded myself of an anti-war demonstration that I'd helped to organize, which had been opened with a First Nations prayer. There is an unwritten rule among the Vancouver Left that, because we are on unceded territory—because aboriginal title to Vancouver and British Columbia has never been relinquished through treaties, with the limited exception of the Nisga'a—we begin each of our events with an acknowledgement of this fact and, whenever possible, open with a First Nations speaker. My favourite of these introductory speeches was given at a fundraiser for the Revolutionary Association of the Women of Afghanistan by Kat Norris, a Coast Salish activist who gave an enriching, expansive autobiographical sketch that complemented the event and expanded its scope. The most nerve-wracking of such introductions was a prayer to open a demonstration at Sunset Beach against the war in Iraq. The speaker began, "Lord Jesus Christ ..." and we, the organizers, began tugging on our collars like cartoon characters. We were being ridiculous. Luckily, the future of Native politics in Vancouver isn't dependent on well-intentioned white folks. Vancouver is home to a generation of brilliant young First Nations leaders, such as curator and artist Tania Willard, who for years was the editor of the magazine *Redwire*; or activist-blogger-prodigy Dustin Rivers, whose intelligence and charisma belie his tender age.

This younger generation of activists seems to move—and lead its allies—back and forth between the urban and rural battlegrounds with increasing ease. In the summer of 2004, an impressive coalition of indigenous and immigrants' rights activists arranged for a contingent of Vancouverites to bus up to the Sun Peaks ski resort just outside of Kamloops in order to buttress a demonstration by the Secwepemc, whose land was being eaten up by the resort. My guilty white heart soared the whole euphoric weekend, especially when one speaker claimed that, in an inversion of classic colonial divide-and-rule tactics, the Natives had "separated the good settlers from the bad." Every twenty-something white radical with patchy blond facial hair aspires to being a good settler.

Given the seeming complexity of the issues in play, in recent months I've been quite taken with the drawings of two First Nations artists for their forthrightness, simplicity, and playfulness. First, two drawings by Mike Dangeli, a dancer and artist and cultural activist who has created two images—in traditional northwest shapes and styles—of the middle finger being flipped at the onlooker. One image is a T-shirt, for sale on Commercial Drive

in red on black, or black on grey; the other is an acrylic-on-canvas painting called *Birdie,* which he says was inspired by his aunt as she drove their group of dancers up the I-5 highway.

The third drawing is one of the unofficial logos for the anti-Olympics campaign, by a First Nations artist who works under the pseudonym Zig Zag. The image, framed inside the slogan "No Olympics on Stolen Native Land," is of a thunderbird perched on the Olympic rings, having ripped one of them open with his beak, and shitting a thunderbolt over them. You don't have to be too well versed in postcolonial deconstruction to be able to enjoy that.

QUÉBÉC

When I was a little kid, the only other French Canadians I ever met in Vancouver were teachers, like my father. Pierre Trudeau's French immersion concept had created a pedagogical gold rush wherever there wasn't a ready supply of Francophones, and *British* Columbia having less Franco to it than a retrospective on Spanish anarchist heroes was the lodestar for any Québécois with a bachelor's degree who wanted to upgrade with a little teacher training. Some of them, like my dad (who had until then been a suit salesman and RCMP dispatch operator), found that all along they'd carried with them an incredible, hidden aptitude for educating, and flourished; others, like my dad's friend Christian (who had been a butcher), were miserable. Going to school in the Lower Mainland over the course of the 1980s and '90s, I had my fair share of the latter and a tiny handful of the former. Still, from childhood, a lesson was driven home:

> Vancouver + French Canadian = Teacher.
> Years later, the equation had changed drastically:
> Vancouver + French Canadian = Squeegee Kid.

By the early years of the new century, whenever I heard the mother tongue of my paternal family being spoken near where I grew up, it wasn't in staff rooms or from in front of chalkboards, but from down on the sidewalk, firing upwards, peppered amongst English-language requests for change.

In October 2002, the *Vancouver Courier* ran a cover feature on the issue of homelessness and drug use among Québécois youth in Vancouver. As with any exposé of racialized hardship, the publication strove for sensitivity, opting for the subtle headline "Coureurs de squeegee." The protagonist of the story was Eric (pronounced Eh-reek, presumably), an unsympathetic French staple-face who enjoyed trips out to Vancouver for heroin and crack in between bouts of sleeping at his mom's in Québec City. The kernel of the piece was the estimation "by local Francophone organizations that one in every four homeless people in Vancouver under 25 is French-Canadian, the majority hailing from Quebec."

Many had arrived, according to the story and corroborating what was at the time conventional wisdom, after working as fruit pickers in the Okanagan. When I first read that, my mind went back to a French girl I once knew named Julie who, after arriving in Vancouver, had found work selling falafels downtown, but who, as a picker, had had her menstrual cycle thrown out of whack from the pesticides. Francophones used to do a lot of fruit picking in BC; so much, actually, that in the 1980s the Canadian Farmworkers Union (the Punjabi-founded and -led labour and anti-racist organization) used to produce some of its literature in French as well as English and Punjabi. These days, it's no longer a popular option for young Québécois, and the work is primarily done by Sikhs, as well as Spanish-speaking migrants from Mexico and South America. But in the days when it was done by youngsters from *la belle province*, the combination of fickle, low-paid seasonal employment, plus the well-documented hostility to young Francophones in the Interior, meant that a lot of poor French kids landed helpless in the city. The changeover from Québécois migrants to other workers has made the once-ubiquitous French squeegee kid an endangered species today.

The *Courier* article also confirmed what I'd already picked up from conversations with my father and cousins and friends: that Vancouver holds a special place in the Québécois imagination. The first French Canadians to settle in the Lower Mainland were the mill workers brought out to Mallairdville, which sits between today's Coquitlam and New Westminster, but there was a darker side to Francophone migration even then. The labourers were brought out in the midst of racist hysteria to replace cheap Sikh labour; the French Canadians were just white enough to placate the racists, just cheap enough to be worth hiring.[47] Several decades later, some critics in Québec argued that in British Columbia, French Canadians were just like any other immigrant group and assimilated to the point of invisibility.[48]

Despite all that, it's not unreasonable for Vancouver to have such a poetic, liberating place in the Québécois imagination that we're the only big city completely outside Canada's history of French-English conflict; we're the major town in the only province without a significant, pre-Confederation Francophone population, and thus the only one without a painful, persecutory history of Orange language laws and cultural bullying (against the French, at least). Just recently, my teenaged cousin in Laval expressed to me his suspicion that everyone in Toronto hates Québec; conversely, a young Québécois can leave for an adventure in Vancouver and not feel like he's surrendering to the bulldogs of chauvinistic federalism or even the anti-French cowboys of the Albertan West. (I once met a French Canadian in Edmonton who asked me, in muted French, if we were safe speaking Canada's other official language.) When he arrived in the mid-1970s, in the aftermath of the FLQ crisis, my dad was able to get a job as a waiter in the Stanley Park Dining Hall despite his lack of English, and he still brags about how much the English people loved his accent, rewarding his missing s's and h's with tips. There's far less cultural baggage for Vancouverites in this respect; the city just doesn't think about Québec all that much, and that can be liberating.

In fact, Québec is so far off the Vancouver map, that when, in 2009, the Vancouver Organizing Committee for the Olympics (VANOC) announced that it was bringing in high-priced Francophones to ensure the bilingualism of the 2010 winter games, it was also announced that they were coming *from France*. Though the Olympics gig is just about the definition of seasonal, I doubt they will stick around after the games. Too bad, really, because I love the idea of a squeegee kid speaking Parisian French. That I'd pay to see, *hostie*.

THE Penth

AFTER GAM
PARTY HQ

PIZZA SLICE $1
VEGE SAMOSA $1

CELEBRIT

Growing up in Burnaby, it is impossible not to be aware that it is the place that gave the world Michael J. Fox. The claim on Fox runs all across Vancouver—the Arts Club Theatre on Granville Island displays old black-and-white pictures of his live stage productions in the Lower Mainland prominently along the wall of its foyer—but in the suburb of Burnaby, where he's *really* from, legends about him abound. When I was a kid, there was an urban legend that at Burnaby Central High School, his desk was encased in glass, displayed prominently in the front entrance; I graduated from Central, and even though the story wasn't true, the myth was so much a part of my imagination that when I remember the entrance and trophy case as they actually were, I automatically imagine the desk, too, and have to edit it out.

Stand-up comics, more than anybody else, I think, have a good idea about what things and which people are truly held sacred by society because we get to see which taboos they'll laugh at when pressed. After Michael Jackson and David Carradine died, there were jokes made immediately (in Jackson's case, within hours) and audiences went for them. Conversely, I have never once seen a comic make a joke in Vancouver about Michael J. Fox's illness—living, as we do, in the era of cheap, shock humour, many have tried—and get away with it, without the audience groaning and even booing and just generally making clear that they weren't coming along. When I was growing up, there was an understanding that the Lower Mainland had given the world a Tragic Fox (Terry, the one-legged runner who died of cancer) and a Triumphant Fox (Michael J.), but now that there's a tragic element to both stories, the two men are almost equally sacrosanct.

In grade eight, I went to high school with Michael J. Fox's nephew, Matthew, and amazingly—*incredibly*, looking back at it—it wasn't something that anybody really made a big deal about. It might have been because the boys from Matthew's elementary feeder school were generally the coolest and most popular once we'd all been amalgamated, and, Matthew's family line being old news to them, we all followed suit. The only time that I can remember breaking the unspoken embargo on getting too worked about it was once, in the cafeteria, when Matthew offered me a cookie, which I fished thankfully and casually out of the Ziploc baggy. Part way through this perfectly serviceable, otherwise unremarkable homemade treat, it occurred to me that Matthew had said that his grandmother had made it.

"Wait a minute," I said, storing half the cookie in my cheek, holding the other in my hand. "These are your *grandma*'s cookies?"

"Yeah," said Matthew.

"Like," I said, my breathing slowing in inverse proportion to my heartbeat's speeding up, "Michael J. Fox's *mom*'s cookies?"

"Yes," he answered, and I was equally thrilled with my detective work as I was with my brush with greatness.

Vancouver's relationship to celebrities is fairly similar to my grade eight class's approach to Matthew—mostly, we're cool and casual, punctuated with slightly embarrassing outbursts of excitement.

There are three categories of celebrity with which Vancouver has a relationship: those from here (Seth Rogen, Ryan Reynolds, Kristin Kreuk, Jason Priestley, Will Sasso, Joshua Jackson, Sarah McLachlan); those with a special relationship to the city, who either keep a home here or continue to come back (Robin Williams, for instance, or Kurt Russell and Goldie Hawn, who took a place in the city at least in part so that their son could train to become a hockey goaltender); and those in town working on a movie (everybody, at some point or another; the most infamous such short-term relationship with the city being Oscar-winner Ben Affleck, whose much ballyhooed relationship with Jennifer Lopez—of "the block" Lopezes—was supposedly ended over photographs of poor behaviour at Vancouver's most upscale strip club, Brandi's). Going back to the early city, two vaudeville stars who would later go on to greater fame in other media performed at one of the city's two Pantages theatres: Stan Laurel and the master of comedy, Charlie Chaplin. Early film star Errol Flynn's death in Vancouver in 1959 has been the subject of rumour and myth since it happened,[49] and I even had one comedian insist to me that the West End restaurant where he hosted a stand-up night had once been a whorehouse, and it was where Errol Flynn had died with one of the hookers before his body was moved to someplace more respectable. (The origin of this version of events is likely the fact that "Flynn dropped in" to the Penthouse Nightclub "the night before he died at a West End apartment in the arms of his seventeen-year-old girlfriend," even though this was before the club "was a flourishing centre of prostitution," in the 1960s.)[50]

A fourth, mini-category consists of celebrities who've made enemies in Vancouver by being dinks: David Duchovny famously alienated the whole city by whining about the rain during his stay here for *The X-Files*, and Robert DeNiro made no friends in Yaletown when he presented a cease-and-desist order to local restaurant DeNiro's, named in his honour by the restaurateur, who had even, apparently, set up a special table for the raging bull in case the actor ever visited. And Dane Cook—the vapid, superstar American stand-up whom comedian Andy Kindler once declared "worse than Hitler, because at least Hitler had a point of view" from the stage of the Media Club on Cambie Street—had a tantrum on the Vancouver Yuk Yuk's stage: when the sound was cut for his having gone over time, he responded by throwing the microphone on the floor. The preposterously talented Vancouver comedian who was supposed to headline the show, Peter Kelamis, was quoted in the *Province* as saying he'd "never seen" anything like it "in eighteen years of comedy."[51] Cook had been in Vancouver filming *Good Luck Chuck*, a movie that earned an aggregated rating of five out of 100 on the popular film review site *Rottentomatoes.com*.

Good Luck Chuck was released in September of 2007, just one month after Seth Rogen's *Superbad*, which was based on the writer/ actor's adolescence in Vancouver (where, as a teenager, Rogen performed prodigious stand-up before leaving for Hollywood). In at least a few of the *Rottentomatoes* pull quotes from reviews of Cook's picture, there are unflattering comparisons to Rogen's; yet another reminder that, as a city, we ought to be at least as proud of our exports as we seem to be of our imports. For the record, I've performed at shows where Rogen's mother was in the audience; I have never had a chance to taste her baking.

Every August, Cates Park, on a beautiful piece of Tsleil-Waututh land just off the waters of Indian Arm, is the home of Under the Volcano, Vancouver's annual day-long festival of music and left-wing politics, named in honour of Malcolm Lowry's book. Always a big draw, the festival invites artists, performers, and speakers from all over. In the summer of 2003, the organizers invited David Hilliard, one of the founding members of the Black Panther Party for Self-Defense; that summer, Hilliard was travelling with the Black Panther Fugitives, a hip hop act that included his son, and both Hilliard and the group were appearing on the main stage at UTV.

In the counter-hegemonic spirit of the festival, Hilliard and the Fugitives were given a chauffeur in the inversed-Driving-Miss-Daisy tradition: me. I had decided to break up the monotony of my summer (I was working as a groundskeeper for a housing complex in Port Moody) by volunteering for the festival, and the job I was given was to pick up the Fugitives from the house they were staying at in Strathcona, pick up David Hilliard from his hotel downtown, take them wherever they wanted to go for a few hours (the younger men wanted desperately to see Vansterdam; the elder was patient), then drive them out to the North Shore in time for their events. We had a great day.

At one point, one of the rappers took a cell phone call from his girlfriend, and I could piece together everything she was asking about Vancouver from listening to his half of the conversation, like a Bob Newhart telephone sketch. I could tell exactly when their relatively mundane chat about the flight, the group's sleeping arrangements, and how pretty the city was turned to demographics: "Huh? Oh. Like, *none*," he laughed. "I mean *none*. It's like, one percent of the population." In a way, he wasn't *that* far off. In fact, 1.1 percent of Metro Vancouverites identify as ethnically African (when allowed to claim more than one ethnic origin), and 5.6 percent identify as Caribbean. But Vancouver's famous lack of blackness—the subject of countless punchlines and the first observation offered by any politically incorrect visitor from Toronto or Montréal or the States—is generally overstated. Of the nearly half of Vancouver that is non-white, 2.4 percent is black, as compared with the 2.6 percent that is Latin American and the 2.9 percent that is Japanese;[52] the 2006 Census found that there were 9,730 Japanese Vancouverites, as compared to 5,290 black Vancouverites.[53] And yet, if you were to ask people inside or outside the city, they would likely identify Vancouver as being very Japanese and not black at all (despite, for one example, the long string of Afro Hair Salons, and Caribbean and Ethiopian restaurants along Commercial Drive). Admittedly, the city hosts a lot of Japanese exchange students who wouldn't be a part of the census, and I'm sure a lot of Korean and Chinese and Filipinos have been entered into the inexpert, anecdotal censuses conducted by white Vancouverites observing the city. Even still, to paraphrase a writer who knew something about the ironies of race, it seems that the reports of the city's Afro-anemia are greatly exaggerated.

My friend Adam Rudder, an academic whose thesis examined this very "invisibility" of Vancouver's black population, opened his study with this paradox: "In a population dominated by white immigrants of British descent, the small black population was hard to miss on the streets or in the places of work or recreation where they might be encountered. And yet, this community so visibly marked by their skin colour is almost entirely invisible in the histories and historical records of the city."[54]

He goes on to argue that "that invisibility was not an accident, or a result of the small numbers of black residents, but," rather, "a predictable outcome of settler colonial histories and a *tactic* used by black residents in order to avoid aggressive white hostility."[55]

"Invisibility" is a poignant choice of words: think how many times you hear "Joe Fortes" in Vancouver—in the names of West End restaurants, libraries, community buildings—versus the number of times that you see the man's picture. I was in my early twenties before I learned that Joe Fortes wasn't a Mediterranean or a Romantic (the mental picture I had of Joe Fortes was a hawk-nosed man with thick, straight white hair combed back) but was, in fact, a barrel-chested, moustachioed, dark-skinned Barbadian. And for a city full of people who can't wait to tell you what buildings *Look Who's Talking* was filmed in or where David Duchovny liked to eat spaghetti while shooting *The X-Files*, very little hay seems to be made about the fact that Jimi Hendrix's family made their home, for years, in the East End (although the Past Tense Vancouver blog has an old *Vancouver Sun* photo of Jimi's dad, Al Hendrix, dancing to Duke Ellington at the Forum).[56]

Vancouver gave the country its first black female public official: Rosemary Brown, who was voted in along with Dave Barrett, the

province's first Jewish and first socialist premier, from East Van.[57] When the Jamaican-born Brown later ran for the leadership of the federal NDP, her candidacy was opposed by Stephen Lewis, among others, who decades later would go on to great acclaim beating his breast about how no one listens to black women in Africa. The 1972 election that brought Brown to the legislature did the same for Emery Barnes, an African American from Louisiana who had played football for the BC Lions.[58] In 2008, Barnes's daughter Constance was elected to the Vancouver school board under the Vision Vancouver banner but, like her fellow Vision politico Tim Stevenson, came under fire for a drunk-driving scandal. Another key black figure of North American progressive politics who makes Vancouver home is Jack O'Dell, the former Communist and trade union militant who became one of Martin Luther King's most trusted advisors in the SCLC, much to the chagrin of the anti-Communist Kennedy brothers, who leaned hard on King to lose O'Dell (along with white activist Stanley Levinson) because of his radical politics. For many years, O'Dell has made his home in Kitsilano.

For such a small group, Vancouver's black communities have made a large cultural contribution to the city, from live theatre and television (for decades, Denis Simpson has been one of the actors most immediately associated with Vancouver) to music (my childhood friend Ndidi Onukwulu has, in recent years, become nothing short of a sensation) to literature. A few years ago, poet Wayde Compton, novelist David Chariandy, and cultural studies academic Karina Vernon founded Commodore Books, billed as "the first and only black literary press in western Canada," was named for the boat that brought the first large group of African Americans to British Columbia from California. So far, the press has published a fantastic book of short stories by the late Fred Booker, a one-woman play by Addena Sumter-Freitag called *Stay Black and Die*, as well as Crawford Killian's seminal work on black British Columbian history, *Go Do Some Great Thing: The Black Pioneers of British Columbia*.

There is much overlap, in terms of both raison d'être and personnel, between Commodore Books and HAMP, the Hogan's Alley Memorial Project, dedicated to preserving and commemorating the memory of the working-class neighbourhood at the edge of Strathcona, next to Chinatown, which was destroyed by the construction of the Georgia Viaduct. Hogan's Alley had been the nucleus of the city's black population, and HAMP has worked for many years to share and to honour this fact.

Hogan's Alley was located just a few blocks from where I picked up the Black Panther Fugitives in Strathcona. In 2007, three years after that day, David Hilliard would visit Vancouver again to participate in an event at the Vancouver East Cultural Centre discussing "black urbanism." There is a picture of him at the event, along with Compton and Vernon and a handful of the other people working to make an important part of Vancouver's story more visible. There's a blonde woman in the photo, but I don't think she's the driver.

POLICE

The notoriously obnoxious marketing line for the new Woodward's development—"Be Bold or Move to Suburbia"—managed to
be simultaneously contemptuous of both the suburbanites priced
out of Vancouver proper by real estate speculation as well as the
neighbourhood's existing, low-income residents, who were reduced
to some kind of safari that had to be faced boldly. Of course, the
Vancouver Police Department will act as game wardens at any such

Do Not linger in
Stairwell- or Police
will be called

safari, with patrols, harassment, and arrests playing a decisive role in managing the excitement, making sure nobody has to be *too* bold.

In its 2009 summer issue, the *Walrus* magazine profiled a new piece by artist Stan Douglas called *Abbott & Cordova,* a painstaking recreation of the 1971 Gastown Riot, during which Vancouver police violently charged a pro-legalization smoke-in "set to be installed [...] in the multimillion-dollar Woodward's building redevelopment." Douglas, who, as the piece notes, "has documented the neighbourhood before" (most notably in the magnificent *Every Building on 100 West Hastings*), thoughtfully explains his new work, while the *Walrus* writer, Leigh Kamping-Carder, intelligently locates the purchase of the piece and the development in which it will feature within the "palimpsest" of the neighbourhood. She concludes: "There was a protest here. And every morning, condo dwellers will pass it on their way to work, their reflections gliding over the image like present-day ghosts."[59] What's left hanging in the air is whether the new condo owners, who will inevitably be at the forefront of demands to "clean up" the neighbourhood by moving loiterers and ticketing jaywalkers and unlicensed street vendors, will see anything but deliverance in the police violence re-created by Douglas.

The BC Civil Liberties Association position paper released after the Gastown riot addresses one of the main concerns still facing the city more than thirty-five years later: civilian oversight of the police.

> An expanded, reconstituted and revitalized Board of Police Commissioners might be able to handle complaints of police abuse, and complaints by police of their own treatment, handle them effectively, and be seen to do so. Failing that, however, [...] serious consideration should be given to the establishment of either a Civilian Review Board or of an Office of Ombudsman which would have responsibility to handle such complaints.[60]

From riot to riot and beating to beating, policing in Vancouver has been an international embarrassment. Former Chief Jamie Graham resigns in the middle of a controversy, then tries to reappear a little while later in Victoria and has to be chased by rights groups; current Chief Jim Chu promises his department won't be trying to get rid of the residents of the DTES before the Olympics, and immediately after the announcement his cops start throwing jaywalking tickets like they're in a ticker-tape parade.

When, in 2005, then-city finance committee chair Tim Louis called the Vancouver Police Department a "rogue department," he meant it fiscally, with reference to the department's tendency for burning through tax dollars.[61] The problem is, the phrase seemed apt for everything else that was going on, too: leaving Frank Paul in an alleyway to die of hypothermia; driving low-level criminals into Stanley Park to beat them up; failing to lift a finger when dozens of aboriginal women began to go missing, but springing into action every time a Native walked through Gastown with a TV.

For a few years, the VPD was the Goofus to the RCMP's Gallant—until the Braidwood Inquiry into the Taser death of Polish immigrant Robert Dziekanski at the Vancouver International Airport. As the testimony became more and more farcical (the revelation that the cops were terrified because Dziekanski was holding a stapler led me to wonder whether Vancouver's notorious gangs could take sanctuary at Office Depot) and the character defects of the officers more pronounced (one was simultaneously dealing

with a vehicular homicide that he'd caused while driving drunk), Vancouverites began to file the incident along with the seemingly endless litany of egregious police actions in the Lower Mainland. You say the cops shot a guy with an X-Acto knife? Makes sense. Erased the video footage on somebody's cell phone? I don't *dis*believe you. The off-duty cop who beat up an immigrant delivering newspapers got three weeks house arrest? Wonder if it would have been a month, even for a white dude.

The one positive offshoot, in this respect, to living in a city like Vancouver is that you get to avoid the nauseating excesses of right-wing cop worship on display in other cities. New York, for instance, is famous for its hyperbole, naming streets for the heroism of

police, selling NYPD caps and T-shirts, and using phases like "the city's finest" without irony. In Vancouver, nobody ever gets on your back about not trusting the cops—nobody, for instance, told anti-Olympics activist Chris Shaw that he was being paranoid when he complained that the VISU (the special force assigned to the Winter Games) had met him at his regular coffee shop, rather than his home or work, in order to intimidate him and show that they'd be watching him. Many Vancouverites just assumed that he was right, because it made sense and it fit a pattern. Even the most conservative, law-and-order fans of the police tend to damn Vancouver law enforcement with faint praise. A 2003 editorial published in the *North Shore News* and posted at *PrimeTimeCrime.com* in defence of the officers who used the cover of Stanley Park to kick some ass bore the headline, "'Stanley Park Six' not evil." *Not evil.* I'm willing to buy that, sure, but it's still a far cry from Vancouver's Finest.

RICH PEOPLE

In my late teens, a very wealthy friend from Winnipeg was in town visiting family friends in the heart of establishment Vancouver on Shaughnessy's famous Angus Drive. (I realized how rich a spot it had to be when I asked my dad where it was and all he did was drop his jaw and repeat the name of the street.) While he was in town, my friend, whom we'll call "K," called and said he wanted to come see me out in Burnaby. I know that dialogue such as the following is only supposed to occur in terrible sitcoms or late Woody Allen films, but I promise that this exchange actually took place:

K.: "What's the fastest way for me to get from Angus Road to where you are?"

Me: "Make a bad investment."

K. thought the line was hilarious, which, in his defence, it was. But he *really* thought it was funny, and I could hear him then share it at the other end of the phone, where it was killing (K. often used to repeat my jokes to his friends and family because he dreamed of representing show business people someday; today, he's with a major Hollywood agency and represents one of the biggest comedy stars on American television).[x] Although they were laughing at the massive socio-economic chasm between us, it didn't even occur to me, at the time, to be offended. They were, after all, in the heart of histori-cal, residential wealth in Vancouver, where "[t]he CPR planned, developed and marketed the Shaughnessy Heights subdivision as an exclusive enclave for the wealthy elite of the growing city."[62]

They were there, and I was in Burnaby, a town once described as "a small city that abuts East Vancouver"[63]—not Vancouver, mind you, but specifically *East Van* (in the 1960s, the possibility of amalgama-tion between the two cities was briefly on the table). Eventually K. made it out to Burnaby, and later on I even trekked back with him to Angus Drive. The house was like nothing I'd ever seen: the kids' rooms were filled with electronics and sports paraphernalia and were stocked to represent that very moment in time, whereas the grown-up parts of the house were timeless, simultaneously under-stated and bullying in their display of riches, and I saw something I'd never seen before but would later read more and more stories about: a silent Filipina lady doing chores in a house full of white people.

Rich people in Vancouver were otherworldly to me (I can dis-tinctly remember my absolute amazement when I found out that, empirically speaking, it really does rain more often in the northeast

x. At a religious function in Winnipeg, K., who is Jewish, once retold a joke I'd made to him about a scene in the Old Testament wherein Zipporah, Moses's wife, circumcises their son and touches the foreskin to his foot; apparently, everyone laughed except for the rabbi, who began a long, painful explanation of why my joke was scripturally incorrect.

quadrant of the city than in the southwest; I had always just assumed that it was a trick of psychology). The city's wealthy had first caught my attention when I was eleven and my angelic, blond, *castrato*-voiced little brother joined the Bach Choir, a children's chorus of singers in red sweaters who often performed with the Vancouver Symphony Orchestra at the Orpheum. (Nobody was particularly surprised when my brother later came out of the closet.) My father and I accompanied him to a Christmas performance at

VANCOUVER HAS SOME VERY RICH PEOPLE. SOME PEOPLE HERE ARE SO RICH THAT THEY GOT TOGETHER TO STAND UP A DEAD TREE THAT FELL OVER IN STANLEY PARK. A DEAD TREE. YOU KNOW HOW THEY STOOD IT UP WHILE THEY RAISED ALL THE MONEY THEY NEEDED? WITH LUMBER! THAT'S AS IF THEY'D KILLED A MAN AND PUT HIS HEART INSIDE AN OLD, DEAD MAN BECAUSE PEOPLE WANT THEIR PICTURE TAKEN WITH THE DEAD MAN. SOME PEOPLE WERE OUTRAGED AT THIS MISSPENT MONEY, SAYING IT COULD HAVE GONE TOWARD HELPING THE HOMELESS PROBLEM IN THIS CITY. SOMEHOW, I DON'T THINK IT CAME DOWN TO THAT DECISION. I DOUBT THAT THOUGHT WAS, "SHOULD I HELP THE HOMELESS OR STAND UP THIS TREE?" I FEEL IT WAS MORE ALONG THE LINES OF "SHOULD I HELP STAND UP THIS TREE OR SHOULD I SHOULD I HAVE KANGAROOS SHIPPED IN FROM AUSTRALIA SO I CAN BOX THEM IN MY BACKYARD?"

GRAHAM CLARK

Oakridge Mall in the winter of 1991, and the shopping centre—being west enough to feel completely foreign to me—was exotically affluent and fancy-pants. This performance was a rare sighting of the wealthy during my childhood, supplemented only by my dad's occasionally taking us for drives out near UBC to look at the mansions. (I'm still not sure what principle these tours operated on. Aspiration? Class antagonism? Or was it simply, given that my father is of the same persuasion as his younger son, a *design* thing?)

Whatever the case, I didn't get another good look at the city's ruling class until I was twenty and started working as a valet. It would have been a strange job for a socialist under any circumstances, but I was in a particularly bitter place, having just failed to gain a first contract at Playdium, the massive arcade in Metrotown Mall, where I'd been working and had led the campaign to organize into the service sector local of the Canadian Autoworkers union (the same local that would later successfully organize the Chapters bookstore on Robson Street). Not that it would have taken long to become embittered anyway: I was working for a parking service contracted out to restaurants and private functions before the bottom fell out from the hi-tech boom, which serviced a wealthy Vancouver still very much in hubristic mode. Especially in Yaletown, it wasn't rare to overhear things like, "That's why you've got to go to the *Third* World" or to see a homeless French Canadian be told, "*Tabernac*—fuck off!" in front of a group of Anglophones or to watch a man turn to his family and laugh after telling a panhandler, "Sure I've got change, but not any I'm going to give to you!" when they'd just finished eating a meal that cost hundreds of dollars.

During my time parking and fetching vehicles for tips from the 604-tunate, I encountered a few notables. I parked a car for then-Canucks hockey coach Marc Crawford, who was very kind but was, that night, coaching against the Montréal Canadiens, and so I said a curse inside his car (I'm sorry to tell you that it worked, and the Habs won in the years since, and my team loyalties began to balance out and have even shifted in favour of the Canucks); I parked the silver Bentley of Peter Brown, Expo 86 finance committee chairman and VANOC board member and all-around gagillionaire; I parked Vancouver-BMW-kingpin Brian Jessel's vehicle, some exceedingly rare beemer that the kitchen staff at C Restaurant were jealous that I got to drive; I parked for Beau Bridges, who was in town filming a movie and apparently loves seafood.

The company's valets parked at rich people's private mansions in the afternoons for children's birthday parties and at night for dinner receptions for world-famous pianists. (Before that particular gig, on Blanca Street down by the water and out near UBC, we were warned by our boss that the female client didn't particularly want us to speak to her and had yelled at a valet the previous year for coming in to tell her that the last car was gone for the night.) Since most of my take-home came from tips, I started working the angles—a particularly demeaning strategy in Vancouver is to not take cover from the rain on wet nights and stoically hold the door

open for the lady without even wincing in the storm, soaked like you just parked the SS *Edmund Fitzgerald*, then run around to the driver's side for your gratuity. I started to feel so humiliated by my job that I would bring heavy-hitter books with me to read outside where the patrons could see me, as though some multimillionaire couple from Point Grey was going to have an epiphany on the way into the Villa Del Lupo—"Did you see that, honey? The valet was reading Gramsci! My whole paradigm's been shifted!"—and I could go home not feeling crummy.

There are several different kinds of rich people in Vancouver. The old money ones in Shaughnessy and Kerrisdale and Point Grey go back a long way—or have the bank balances to make up the distance if they don't—and there's no shaking them; they're world-class rich and will go toe-to-toe with Bridle Path or Westmount any day. In Dunbar, their status is less secure, which might have played a role in the recent controversy that erupted when it was discovered that the Dunbar Residents Association was instructing members to phone 9-1-1 if they saw a street person in the neighbourhood. Then there are homesteading rich folks establishing beachheads in "up-and-coming" neighbourhoods like Gastown, Strathcona, the Drive, and Hastings-Sunrise. The wealthy in those neighbourhoods have thick-plastic-rimmed glasses and enjoy cycling and are never more than a few months away from feeling entitled to start sculpting their new neighbourhood in their image.

But throughout downtown, there's a lower rung of seemingly rich folk that's treading water, people who are condo-poor, laying out everything they've got to live in Yaletown or Coal Harbour on the promise that owning one of the tiny boxes in those neighbour-hoods is the key to long-term security. Though they seem to be the ones most culturally distinct from working- and lower-middle-class Vancouverites, with their distressed jeans and their yoga pants and their indoor sunglasses, they just might be, ultimately, the easiest ones to relate to on that side of the line.

One of the ironies of the Vancouver-as-Lotusland image that lets the rest of Canada dismiss the city as a sort of crushed-lavender nest of gentle hippies, not to mention the irony of Vancouver's sense of superiority when it comes to the Calgary-style right-wing stew of neo-conservative politics and neo-liberal economics reigning in Alberta and rural BC, is that since the mid-1970s our city has been home to the wacky-rightist mothership: the Fraser Institute. Since forming with the support of the forestry industry to derail BC's first socialist premier, Dave Barrett,[64] and named in honour of the river it would no doubt like to see privatized, the Fraser Institute has been the clearest manifestation of class consciousness in Vancouver: an intellectual self-defence club for the rich. (VANOC's Peter Brown, whose Bentley I parked, is on the board of trustees.)

Unlike many right-wing organizations in North America, the Fraser Institute makes no bones about its social preferences; although occasionally throwing a populist sop to tax-enraged suburbanites, the FI doesn't pretend to be about empowering BC Lions fans and church-goers. Stunts like their publication of questionable school rankings nakedly empower those who have the resources to move their children to a richer school and sabotage the most vulnerable institutions by drawing away students and, consequently, the funding that comes with them. The FI likes money and the people who have it.

Put another way: in order to get to the elevator that brings you to the offices of the Fraser Institute, you have to go through a Lexus dealership. (To be fair, the offices of the *Georgia Straight* used to be in there, too; but while the *Straight*'s environment was cute irony, with the FI you get a distinct "Boys-this-is-what-we're-fighting-for" feeling.) In June 2007, when I visited, the offices were resplendent with framed photographs of long-since-discredited fellow-travellers like former Ontario Premier Mike Harris (if the FI really wanted to put its money where its less-regulation mouth is, it would bring in bottled water from Walkerton) and Conrad Black (I wish they'd sent him to a *real* prison where, at the very least, he'd have had to fight to keep the nickname Lord Black). The day I was there, the guest speaker was given an Adam Smith tie—a plus for any stockbroker whose office isn't high enough to jump out of in the event of a market crash.

This essay began with a piece of real dialogue seemingly too contrived to have actually happened, so I'll bookend it with another. Although it seems impossibly perfect, the following exchange occurred between me and a Fraser Institute regular:

Me: "Excuse me, how do I get to the bathroom?"

Him (pointing down the hallway): "Just keep to the right."

I suppose that's one way to end up in the toilet.

Despite the cheap pizza on every corner and a city-full of pot-massaged appetites, a fat guy can never really feel completely a part of Vancouver; in a city so defined by nature, full-fledged citizenship is predicated upon the active, red-blooded enjoyment of every rock face and tree, bike trail and sea wall. I used to live near Commercial Drive with two out-of-towners—one a compact, sinewy Haligonian, the other a lanky Pole with a massive outgrowth of hair—each harbouring a pagan-level commitment to the outdoors and its constant appreciation; the Pole had even set himself to the task of building a bike trailer for his canoe. Conversely, I use the mountains almost exclusively for finding north (like many Vancouverites, I'm helplessly lost in other cities without the massive, snow-capped compass I've grown up with), and as a result, despite my being the only local, I felt distinctly less Vancouverish than they seemed.

The same thing happens for the fat guy in Mountain Equipment Co-Op—the place that comedian Paul Breau accused Vancouverites of turning toward in unison to pray (his first hint was the sign on the side of the building: "MEC.ca"). At MEC, the preponderance of rosy-cheeked, athletic *Übermenschen* excited to get outside and into the wholesome, taut-muscled labour of camping and their profound relationship with the soil makes us largely sedentary, endomorphic types feel distinctly like Alvy Singer in a room full of Maxes. I made a trip to MEC once with my friend Dwayne—an avid cyclist, kayaker, and Ontario expat who lived in the bushes off Jericho Beach when he first arrived in Vancouver decades ago—and he watched in confusion as I shrunk into myself, suddenly nervous and uncomfortable, hyperconscious of my weight, amply aware of everywhere I was ample. Eventually, though, I got on my bike, and—still pumpkin-figured—was able to get in on some of the action, particularly appreciating the almost absurd beauty of False Creek, which miraculously runs right into the very centre of the city.

Physically embarking upon the topography of the city and its surrounding areas seems to be a way for Vancouverites to actively engage a beauty that we might otherwise experience passively—in that sense, we're like a very pretty girl training to be good at running or sports as a way of taking control over a physicality that might otherwise be used to define *her*. Someone told me that Sinead

I LOVE WHEN IT RAINS IN VANCOUVER. LOVE IT. JUST THE THOUGHT OF A MANSION SLIDING OFF THE SIDE OF A HILL TICKLES ME INSIDE. EVERY TIME A MANSION FALLS IN VANCOUVER AN ANGEL GETS ITS WINGS.

ROB PUE

O'Connor shaved her head because with hair she was too beautiful to be taken seriously, and whether or not that's true, it reminds me of Vancouver, a city that wants its looks to be noticed, but frets that its prettiness will ultimately get in the way whenever it wants to be taken seriously by people in bigger, heavier, more historical cities like Toronto or New York or anyplace in Europe. In July 2009, the *Tyee* website published a more-than-slightly insecure reflection on whether Vancouver could make the most of its international spotlight during the Olympic Games. Titled "Vancouver's 'Brand': Ski Bums or Green Brainiacs?," the essay made the city sound like an attractive job interviewee nervously deciding between closing and opening the second button on his shirt before going into the office:

> Now imagine you're a city on the move. You're full of great ideas about how cities should be run. You're innovative, free-thinking. Sure, you're graced with spectacular scenery and everyone loves a handsome city, but you're a bit more than that. That's what you tell yourself. [...] And with the world's eyes on you, you could make the pitch: "I'm a Pacific Rim leader! I'm a model of sustainable urbanism! You could learn a thing or two from me!" And does the world listen? Or is it too busy admiring white-capped waves, reflected in your steel-glass towers, and the soaring mountains behind?[65]

The *Tyee* is an online publication that, though very much emblematic of the post-modern, contemporary Vancouver of ideas, also draws on the iconography of nature, taking its name from a local species of salmon (the website bills itself justifiably as "a feisty one online," and its subsidiary blog about politics is, cutely and correspondingly, named the Hook). The word "tyee" also appears frequently (in its Chinook-jargon context meaning variously chief or deity, depending on how it's qualified) in the first literary work that set out to fuse the essence of the city with its natural environs, E. Pauline Johnson's 1911 publication, *Legends of Vancouver,* a collection of interpreted Squamish legends initially written for the *Province.* (Even back then the *Province* was a conservative paper, but it's worth reflecting on the fact that almost a century ago the paper gave space to a female, First Nations writer sharing her take on local Native mythology; today, you won't find much more in there than pavement populism, right-wing panic, reviews of American movies, and puns built around professional sports.) *Legends of Vancouver* vivifies already breathtaking features of the city's landscape, like Stanley Park's incredible Siwash Rock—a jutting heap of stone that really, *really* does look like an old native chief wrapped in a blanket. Johnson also shares the story of the two most famous points on the Vancouver horizon:

> You can see them as you look towards the north and the west, where the dream-hills swim into the sky amid their ever-drifting clouds of pearl and grey. They catch the earliest hint of sunrise, they hold the last colour of the sunset. Twin mountains they are, lifting their twin peaks above the fairest city in all Canada, and known throughout the British Empire as "The Lions of Vancouver."[66]

With care and patience, Johnson frames the act of naming and the power that comes with it—the importance of which is realized particularly sharply in the colonized world, one of the reasons why it was so important for Palestine's national poet, Mahmoud Darwish, to state in his "Poem of the Land": "I name the soil I call it/an extension of my soul."[67] Everywhere that the map was pink, the two peaks were known as the Lions (of course they would be called that, or else something like it, the Fox and the Fiddle maybe, or the Tea and the Crumpet). But Johnson, in the name of Chief Joe Capilano and his people, doesn't call them that—she calls them the Two Sisters and the Chief's Daughters, two great peacemakers who bring an end to inter-nation warfare along the coast and are rewarded with the immortality that comes with being turned to stone and lifted atop a mountain. (Siwash Rock, too, comes about through the seemingly dubious reward of becoming stone, which just goes to show you that one mythologist's Medusa victim is another man's grand-prize winner.) The gulf between seeing two lions or two treaty-making girls in the same twin mounds of rock is a reminder that, though we're all presented with an identical geography, we take it in differently. Some see in our landscape a challenge to climb up it, then ski down it; for my part, beyond asking it for directions, I'm happy just to have it look pretty, cuddling my city up against the water.

Nature, in turn, gets to shape the kind of city, and city-dwellers, who are taking it in. In his book *Dream City*, Lance Berelowitz lays it out: "Almost everything about Vancouver springs from this formulation of geographical facts: the quality of the air, the taste of the water, the light, the smells, the colours of the landscape, the food it grows and eats, the very climate and resulting lifestyle. This is Vancouver's *genius loci*. And the city's urban form has responded to these elements."[68]

In Vancouver, you never get the sense that you sometimes get when you're in Toronto of an abiding, earnest, untrammelled secular humanism and belief in a purely anthropocentric urbanism. Driving through Hogtown, nature seems to occur incidentally, and sometimes all you can see in any given direction are miracles of human ingenuity. But Berelowitz is right about Vancouver: nature is dominant in every frame ever taken of the city, insinuating itself into Vancouver's life like an all-powerful parent, and since the only thing you can do with an all-powerful parent is worship him or kill him, it's no surprise that we're a city polarized between histories of ecological movements and resource-extraction capitalism.

There's an old socialist-realist mural in the auditorium of the Maritime Labour Centre down by the water on Triumph Street in East Van that pays tribute to the labour history of the city in images of shipbuilding, merchant seafaring, and lumber mills. (Actually, Vancouver's celebrated photographer Stan Douglas has a beautiful photograph of the piece towering above a dais and several rows of empty seats, as though right before a left-wing talk.) I remember standing in that auditorium next to a middle-aged, ex-Trotskyist, still-lefty friend before he turned to me suddenly and, out of nowhere, said, "God, I hate that fucking mural." Having always liked it myself, if not necessarily appreciating it artistically, I asked him why. He moved through the piece from left to right, pointing out the environmental abomination of each of the industrial activities depicted. Suddenly I realized that in both corners of the mural, clouds of toxins are billowing proudly out of smokestacks into the air.

Vancouver is, predictably, one of the first North American cities to see environmentalism enter the mainstream. The city's vibrant countercultural, anti-war, anti-nuclear movements of the late 1960s and early 1970s gave the world the international phenomenon known as Greenpeace, whose story is told in a book of the same name by writer and activist Rex Weyler. The city also gave the world David Suzuki—though not without first doing its best to try and disown him through racism and internment. Suzuki and his family were taken from their Marpole home during World War II, but despite this betrayal he has remained committed to the city, living for decades in Point Grey; it's not unusual to see him shopping at the farmers' market on Granville Island. Local movements like Greenpeace and Suzuki's half-fiery, half-patient exhortations to environmental responsibility have shaped the politics of the province and of the city, sometimes finding common cause with First Nations rights activists—such as in Clayoquot Sound in 1993, the high water mark for Canadian civil disobedience, participation in which is still worn as a badge of honour by many Vancouver activists.

But if ecological politics in the city have injected themselves into the mainstream, the mainstream, too, has set to work diluting ecological movements. Where Greenpeace once exemplified bold, direct action and environmental self-defence, a Vancouverite today is most likely to encounter Greenpeace in the form of a mock-enthusiastic paid canvasser (emails even floated around years ago about the organization's effort to break the canvassers' union). And while Rex Weyler has continued to follow and promote social justice and aboriginal rights (not to mention writing a book about the teachings of Jesus), other early Vancouver Greenpeace pioneers like Paul Watson have gone off the rails; he now produces a whale-defence reality TV show and spouts chauvinistic sentiments about the Japanese as well as Native whaling communities like the Makah in Neah Bay, Washington.

For his part, Suzuki seems to have relaxed his socialism in the hopes of eking some minor concessions to climate Armageddon, like carbon offsets for the Olympic Games. In June 2009, Suzuki—once a vociferous critic of corporate avarice and its sundry misuses of science and the environment—championed Save-on-Foods and the Overwaitea Food Group for their partnership on the SeaChoice program, which encourages more-sustainable commercial seafood practices. Overwaitea is owned by Jimmy Pattison, a man who built his empire on, among other things, car sales, trucking, commercial fishing, and other resource extraction; the two political sides of Vancouver's dialectic are now standing behind the same podium.

As for me, I'm not sure I trust Save-on-Foods to save the earth; they played a big role in making me too fat to appreciate nature properly in the first place.

POT

When we were fifteen years old, my friend B. and I decided that we should start growing our own pot. We were on a field trip with our English class down at the Vancouver Playhouse for the afternoon, and rather than trundling like squares back on to the eastbound SkyTrain after the show with the rest of the sheep, we opted, like precocious beatniks, for the gritty romance of Hastings Street, where the BC Bud store had recently been opened, then raided for selling marijuana seeds.

Today, the whole block—known as Little Amsterdam or Vansterdam—is choc-a-bong with head shops and sundry pot para-phernalia, including BC Bud, marijuana activist Marc Emery's flagship store. But back then, the open weed culture was just starting to bud, along with some shake in the form of storefronts specializing in rock T-shirts but supplementing business by dealing in glass pipes and dugouts (also known as "one-hit wonders": small, wooden boxes with two compartments, one to hold loosely cut weed, the other a narrow, spring-loaded cylinder holding a straight metal pipe painted to look like a cigarette, but with a sharp bowl at the end perfect for holding one drag's worth of pot). The BC Bud store was thrilling in its combination of openness and illicitness, like a porn shop, right there on the street for anybody to see, but inside somehow sheltered and secure. The place smelled like hemp and incense, and the staff was notably easygoing, even when a fat teenager approached the cashier to ask if he could buy some seeds.

"Oh, we don't sell seeds here anymore," the short-haired bru-nette told me. This was like a quick punch to the stomach; the seeds—the sale of which had been at the heart of the young busi-ness's notoriety—were the whole reason that B. and I had made the trip. We had seemingly missed the tiny window during which this awesome thing had happened—like hipsters who moved to Vancou-ver just two weeks after the Sugar Refinery closed.

"But," she continued, handing me a business card, "you may want to check out these guys." The flimsy, beige paper card read simply "Terdan Industries,"[xi] alongside an office number and address in the neighbourhood. "They might be able to help you." (The cryptic but largely comprehensible jargon of Vansterdam is still around today, a vague, uncommitted, nominal attempt to duck cops, as well as to establish plausible deniability. A few years ago I was helping a visiting, elderly American poet staying at my

xi. Fake name to protect the real one, not that it'd still be used.

apartment, who suffered from glaucoma, to buy some pot and couldn't find a walk-up dealer that used to be in the area. When I asked a staff person at one of the pot cafés where they'd moved to, an exasperating, two-minute cat-and-mouse conversation ensued that finally ended with, "I don't know what to tell you, man; I can't help. Maybe if you went, like, outside and then around the corner and then downstairs[xii] somebody could help you." Somebody could, in fact, and we waited in line with a bunch of hippies while UFC-looking thugs lorded over a massive stash of bud.)

B. and I found Terdan's office easily but stood outside in the hallway for what seemed like forever. We had a terrified debate over whether we were being set up to be arrested in a sting, and over what sort of violent low-life might be inside. I'm not sure that we ever would have knocked on the door except that a conversation was clearly ending inside, and the door began to open on its own. Someone blew past us, and with trepidation we moved inside.

There, behind a desk, was a giggling, mellow-biker-looking dude with longish, feathered silver hair, a moustache, and shades. He was wearing jeans, a black leather vest, and a broad smile, and he welcomed us into his office. Now, I really should emphasize here that when I was fifteen, I looked about thirteen; there is no way that any of these people mistook us for young adults. B. was in the throes of puberty's gangliest, most teeth-bracing stages, and I was so doughy as to be circular, with a silken blond mushroom cut like the shortstop on a lesbian softball team. We told him what we wanted, and he produced a tiny envelope marked "BC Bud Mix." He told us what it would yield, explaining the pedigree of the bud, plus promising us with a laugh "the best fuckin' shake you'll ever have in your life." We were two or three bucks short of the asking price, but he waved it off and took the money. We thanked him, took the seeds, and began to leave. But he stopped us. Turned out he had something important to show us.

The silver-haired dealer stood up, popped a tape into the VCR, and then sat down behind his desk. The video, filmed inside a grow-op, was hosted by a pedagogue who, for legal and publicity reasons, wore a T-shirt wrapped around his head *fedayee*-style.

"This guy sort of looks like a terrorist," I joked nervously, and, I swear to God, the dealer laughed at that stupid, stammering non-observation more sincerely and more joyously than anyone has ever

WE LOVE OUR POT IN VANCOUVER. WE ARE POT CONNOISSEURS IN VANCOUVER. AND THE POT CONNOISSEURS USED TO GO, "(*INHALE*) COLOMBIA … (*INHALE*) MEXICO …" NOW WE GO, "(*INHALE*) 49TH AND FRASER …"

RICHARD LETT

xii. Fake directions to protect the real ones, not that they'd still be good.

laughed at anything I've ever said. He laughed like a baby does at a funny face, with amazement and discovery. I tell jokes for a living and dream of one day eliciting a similar response from *anybody*.

B. and I never did get to smoke any homegrown weed. After germinating the first seed in a damp paper towel in a jar in my closet, we planted it so far into the forested ravine near my house so that no one would find it, that we never could. (I used to fantasize that the whole 2009 Lower Mainland gang war was being fought over the cartoonishly giant plant we had abandoned.) A few weeks later, my dad and brother accidentally stumbled upon the labelled envelope and vial containing the remaining seeds when, as a treat, they decided to surprise me by cleaning my room; the evidence had been tucked into a toque in my desk drawer and had flown out when they opened it. My dad was mortified—he had never wanted to be the parent who went through his son's bedroom looking for contraband—and felt his goodwill gesture had backfired. (I must have been the only teenager in the world to have his dad *apologize* for having found the beginnings of a grow-op in his room.) Pointedly, he didn't tell me what I had to do, but rather calmly explained the big legal distinction between having some grass (Dad always calls it "grass," and so I'm stuck with the anachronism) and growing it; I told him I understood, and, solemn-faced, I poured the remaining seeds down the toilet like dead goldfish. It was my first, and last, chance at being a millionaire.

Though marijuana is the laziest trope of superficial conversation about Vancouver, the city's pre-eminent cliché, it's hard to avoid. Like most clichés, it starts from a kernel of truth; *unlike* most clichés, it continues from that kernel to be completely true, through and through, to the very extremes of exaggeration and absurdity. Yes, every Vancouverite has smoked up out-of-town visitors to *hashashin* levels of intoxication on a paltry amount that wouldn't even have buzzed them at home. When I was in university, a British Palestinian guest on his way home complained that we were sharing only one joint between five people; hours later, and after we'd thrown away the last third of the smoke, he was panicking about how he'd ever get through customs with his Muslim name if he were *this* terrifyingly high. Touring performers occasionally shit the bed onstage because they overshoot on Vancouver's equivalent of Maine lobsters or Champagne champagne. Once, an vansterdam 42010

attractive female friend of mine was invited backstage at the show of a famous American hip hop act; though the crowd was being told—with great fuck-the-man gusto and to indignant cheers of solidarity—that the rapper was being held up at customs by racist officials, my friend reported from backstage that he was simply waiting in the green room for his weed connection.

In an August 2009 *Vanity Fair* profile of failed Vice Presidential candidate Sarah Palin, writer Todd S. Purdum described Alaska as a place where "it is possible to be both a conservative Republican and a pothead."[69] Similarly, in Vancouver, pot has no power as a cultural signifier, having lost any semiotic potency because of its omnipresence (an omnipresence due, ironically, to a deliberately engineered potency of a different kind). In other parts of the world, smoking pot marks you alternately as a bohemian or a slacker, a free spirit, an outlaw, or a Rastafarian. In Vancouver, you're just as likely to see a spiky-haired commerce student getting high as a dreadlocked skateboarder or an anti-war activist or somebody's right-wing dad. It's around from childhood; my little brother begged his way into his first session with a friend and me when he was twelve. Adolescent recreations and cruelties are built around it, too; some of the popular boys from my school gave me Red Rose tea to smoke at a junior high grad party on the correct assumption that I would humiliate myself by still acting as though I were high—in my defence, I really did feel *something*.

Pot is to Vancouverites what beer is to all Canadians. Yes, it's a tired, irritating cliché that we bristle against when it's used to reduce us to a two-dimensional joke. But it really is stronger here and very good and the nucleus of myriad nostalgic anecdotes and likely to be at any major social function and an important part of a broad social culture and a big problem for American prohibitionists. The major difference between beer culture and pot culture, I guess, is that taking back your cans and bottles can help the planet, whereas recycling your roaches is still an eminently selfish pursuit.

CRIME

Years ago, standing on Kingsway, I wanted to send an email and set about finding some place with Internet. After walking a few blocks, trying the lobbies of ugly motels that Vancouverites have trouble imagining any tourist staying in, I finally found a storefront marked Internet Café on its tinted front windows that was set back from the sidewalk in a building shared with a pizzeria. Though the outside was nondescript (likely by design, as it turns out), the inside was a hard-edged, self-possessed universe. The place was like some sort of interior-design netherworld, a chaotic pit with no light from outside or any sense of the busy street not ten feet from the door, with a massive round table on one side of the room and two computers pushed up against the opposite wall. The woman working there didn't greet me so much as discover me, her face twisted in stunned bewilderment, like I'd come upon her in her living room uninvited.

"Hi," I ventured. "Um, can I use one of the computers?"

"Huh? Oh," she said, suddenly piecing together why I had come into her Internet café. "Yes, hold on." A child was sitting at one of the computers, so she tried booting up the other, but it didn't work. She moved the boy from the working console and, still holding him, pointed at it. "You can use this one."

Slowly, I started to take in the room—not only was there a large table in it, but it was surrounded. By men. Playing cards. And smoking … *indoors*! What should have been obvious from the moment that I saw the place only then occurred to me—this was just as much a circus or a boxing gym as it was a place to check your email; just like the countless Vancouverites who have haplessly walked into bakeries with no cookies or restaurants with no menus, I had stumbled into a front without seeing the signs (opaque windows are always a giveaway; just like signs directing clients to a "discreet back door" on any mirrored-glass shiatsu clinic—nobody's *that* embarrassed about tennis elbow).

There's an episode of *The Simpsons* in which Homer manages, through a combination of pandering and lying and cutting the brake lines on his opponent's car, to get himself elected garbage commissioner of Springfield, only to blow through his annual budget within the first few days. Desperate, he makes up the budget shortfall by selling space under the city to other towns looking to offload their refuse. Pretty soon, the garbage starts popping up in unexpected places, rumbling under the grass and even firing out of the holes on golf courses. I bring it up because the subterranean ubiquity of garbage in Springfield has an analogue in the dirty money—particularly drug money—that surges just underneath the veneer of Vancouver's "legit" economy, popping up in equally unexpected places.

Drug money is the unknown variable in almost any economic equation that you can't otherwise reconcile in Vancouver. Every circle you can't square—that steakhouse you've never seen anybody go into; that computer store with the blinds always shut—gets its corners from the massive, officially unaccounted for economy represented by BC's most famous crop. There's at least as much money in the city from drugs as there is from forestry, and when you start to piece together how much shadow-play there is in Vancouver capitalism, you realize that, essentially, we're Calgary in a world where oil is illegal.

VANCOUVER HAS BEEN DELUGED WITH GANG VIOLENCE. ALMOST NONE OF IT URBAN. WE'VE BECOME THE ONLY CITY ON EARTH WHERE THE INNER CITY IS ACTUALLY THE SAFE ZONE, AND THE SUBURBS ARE CUL-DE-SAC MURDER FIELDS. JUST A BUNCH OF PEOPLE ANGRY THAT ALL THEIR STREETS END IN CIRCLES. THEY'D RATHER SHOOT THEIR WAY THROUGH THAN TURN AROUND AND GO THE LONG WAY TO BUY MILK.

JY HARRIS

In the heart of the city's storied Downtown Eastside, on Cordova Street right next to the Vancouver Police Department (though organizationally independent of it), is the Vancouver Police Museum, a fantastic little walk-up housed in what used to be a real courthouse, then a pretend courthouse for American TV shows like *MacGyver* and *21 Jump Street*. The museum is a gem, filled with incredible photographs like the black-and-white of three female cops squinting into a firing range, revolvers cocked, or the shot of two more female officers dressed like hookers to go undercover for the "Morality Squad." (The latter reminded me of how proud I was when I spotted a sting operation on Victoria Drive near the waterfront, feeling suspicious about the woman standing on the corner in fishnet stockings, and having those suspicions confirmed when I passed the street again on my way back home and watched the cops cuffing a would-be john.)

The museum has other exhibits, too: a re-created morgue with formaldehyde preserves full of bullet-rent hearts and at least two fetuses; a decades-old, cherry-red, police-issue Harley-Davidson; a mannequin in full, old-school VPD pipe-band regalia, including leopard print; a display of loaded dice, underground hockey-pool cards, and illegal Chinese gambling games; as well as documents and timelines outlining the history of crime and policing in Vancouver. There is a tribute wall to the sixteen officers who've fallen in the line of duty in the department's history, which includes a photo of Chief Malcolm MacLennan, who became chief in 1914 and who, as the museum's curators explain elsewhere, "lobbied politicians, with no success, for the medical treatment of drug addicts instead of criminal reprimand." MacLennan also ended the use of prison labour to clear land[70] the same year that he was killed in a Hogan's Alley showdown with an African American police informant named Robert Tait.[71]

Besides its history of angry and often-violent radical politics, the thing about Vancouver that most contradicts its designation as Lotus Land is the violent history of its underworld. Vancouver's placid kayaks and green tea gelatos are the last things that come to mind looking at the museum's wall casing full of confiscated weapons—a display that includes, but is not limited to: truncheons, brass knuckles, knives, ninja throwing stars, medieval maces, improvised flails made from hockey tape and chainsaw chains, blow dart guns, crossbows, sais, nunchuks, studded leather gloves, and samurai swords (the zip guns are in another room). This is the debris left by the broken, terrifying, and terrified layer of brute violence in Vancouver captured by authors like Clint Burnham in *Airborne Photo* and Eden Robinson in *Blood Sports*, or else by Chris Haddock and his army of writers and actors for *Da Vinci's Inquest*.

It's not that it's impossible to reconcile the city's new-age vibe to some of its grisly outbursts of psychopathy. The idea of a flaky, West Coast hamlet marbled with the stories of blood-curdling insanity is an easy one to entertain (Woody Allen perceived California in *Annie Hall* as bouncing between the two poles of health food and the Manson Family murders). To this end, John Melvin Ritchley's gruesome crimes in the West End in 1969—killing one man and

putting his body in a trunk for three weeks while he kept another as a sexual prisoner—fit the profile of the beachfront town; indeed, in the display case for the crime at the Police Museum, the accompanying photo of the neighbourhood, with its soft Technicolors just slightly blurred, makes the crimes seem almost inevitable. Vancouver has had other sensational killings in the California mould—the axe murder of almost the entire Kosburg family by its eldest son, for instance, in 1965 (the museum's display write-up explicitly draws the visitor's attention to "a fine blonde hair" that "can still be seen on the blade from these gruesome murders"), or the Janet Smith murder of 1925, which cast a shadow on Vancouver's financial elite as well as becoming a banner event in the city's history of scapegoating the Chinese, with the kidnapping and torture of Wong Foon Sing (a watershed incident in the history of Vancouver racism, discussed on page 218).

Less reconcilable to the ideal of the city held by Vancouverites and many others is the violence of the organized, systematic, profit-making crime in the city, though the dramatic bloodshed that accompanies our black market has begun to assert itself in terms of shaping perceptions of Vancouver. In a May 2009 article subtly headlined "British Columbia or Colombia," the *Economist* magazine sounded the alarm over the city's gun violence over drug profits. Coming, as it did, less than a year before the Olympic Games, the province and the city sprung immediately into a defence of Vancouver's reputation with an energy and zeal they seemingly hadn't been able to muster to defend its citizens.

But the *Economist* staffers weren't the first Britons to call out the city on its seemingly unstoppable gang problem. In his book about international organized crime in the era of globalization, *McMafia*, Misha Glenny explores some of the hot spots around the world where the chaos wrought by organized crime presents serious obstacles to peace: the nearly lawless frontiers of the former Soviet Union, the streets and prisons of São Paulo, the sex-slave trade routes of the Middle East, the port of Vancouver. Glenny makes the assertion—denied by many in Vancouver—that biker gangs just as organizationally disciplined and impenetrable as the Chinese Triads[72] control the port, which happens to be the most active one in the country. The *Economist* echoed his assessment: "Vancouver has become a distribution hub in a global drugs trade stretching to Asia

and Europe. Local gangs ship out cannabis, amphetamines, and ecstasy made in BC, importing cocaine, heroin, and guns for the Canadian market. Around 135 gangs are thought to be fighting over a business worth an estimated C$7 billion ($6.2 billion) a year."[73]

The structure of the city's economy has always lent itself to crime—particularly vice crime, as the Vancouver Police Museum's popular Sins of the City walking tour emphasizes. The tour, which brings in the vast majority of the museum's funding, begins outside of the St James Anglican church, down the street from the ghosts of the Hastings Mill, where participants are informed that the city we live in today grew out of the desire to sell booze and sex to the men who worked there (and that the resulting Wild West partying that took place was so intense that there were noise complaints from the North Shore).

Huge swaths of Gastown, Chinatown, and Japantown in those early years amounted to a multicultural vice district, with the million stories that one would expect; my favourite is the one recounted in historian Daniel Francis's book *Red Light Neon: A History of Vancouver's Sex Trade*, about a Japanese madame named Kiyoko Tanaka-Goto, who operated two brothels in the area during the 1920s and '30s, one on Powell Street (which she owned with three other women), the other on West Hastings, which belonged to her alone. Though the Asian fetish that white men in Vancouver are notorious for harbouring is thought to be a relatively recent development, as Tanaka-Goto explained, "Those days you could get a white woman for $2 and a Japanese woman for $3 to $5. The Japanese women cost most because they were more in demand."[74] Like most of Japantown, Tanaka-Goto's business came to an end with Japanese-Canadian internment during World War II.

Crime in Vancouver has always been viewed through a racial lens—except, of course, when the criminals are white. The Hells Angels are never called a "white gang," nor are the Bacon brothers (the most colourful crime brothers to hit the Lower Mainland since the Filipponis, who ran the Penthouse night club, but possessing none of what made the latter interesting) ever referred to as "Euro-Canadian." Criminals of Latin American, East Asian, Native, or, especially, South Asian descent, however, will always have their organizations qualified in the newspaper with an adjective indicating racial origin (recently, a multiracial gang calling itself the

United Nations, like some satirical, nightmare version of Trudeau's ideal, has made it more difficult for the city's wags to ascribe violence and criminality to ethnic heritage). That particular Vancouver tradition goes back to one of the area's first agents of colonial law enforcement, Tomkins Brew, who wrote an 1869 letter to the colonial secretary successfully begging for a lock-up to be built "on the lower narrows" which could also be used as a courthouse. Brew's letter is obsessively preoccupied with the area's aboriginal inhabitants: "The inlet is a scene of drunkenness and savage violence on the part of the Indians, they continually threaten the lives of the Whitemen," he writes, before adding, from his position of ethnographic expertise, that "[t]he Indians on the Burrard Inlet are not natives of the place, but recent squatters from Howe Sound." Even if this were true, one struggles to figure how someone arriving from Howe Sound would have less a claim to Vancouver than someone from Britain. Luckily, Brew's letter was the last known incident of police racism toward Natives in the city.[xiii] Actually, the Vancouver Police Department wouldn't hire its first aboriginal officer until 1987, the year the city turned 101.

Natives, of course, were not the only group singled out by police; the country's very first narcotics laws were born out of anti-Chinese racism in the aftermath of Vancouver's 1907 anti-Asian riot, when cabinet minister William Lyon Mackenzie King refused to compensate the opium dealers whose (perfectly legal) concerns had been destroyed. (On the Sins of the City walking tour, Mathieson, who also used to work at the Sun Yat-sen Gardens, is quick to point out the irony of a British Dominion's fear that the Chinese would corrupt their society with opium after the British foisted it onto the Chinese in the first place.)

The spate of gangland killings that riddled Vancouver and its suburbs in late 2008 and early 2009 led to one of those rare moments that we have once every generation, when the low-level violence gets constant enough that the city has to at least pretend it's going to have a conversation about how to address it. The options being put forward by politicians, media, and the citizenry itself are wide-ranging, representing myriad philosophical approaches to social policy, some complementary, some contradictory: mandatory sentencing for gun crimes, harsher drug penalties, longer prison sentences, an end to two-for-one deals (in which time spent in jail

xiii. Do you find that sarcasm sometimes gets lost in print?

before sentencing is worth twice that spent in prison afterwards), partial decriminalization, total decriminalization, legalization, better gang-prevention programs.

Historically, in the fight against the drug and sex trades specifically, the police tend to push down hard on those at the bottom, and the results are disastrous. Daniel Francis makes the convincing case that the sex trade in Vancouver was largely manageable when it was being run out of the Filipponi brothers' Penthouse club, where working girls could keep tabs on each other and johns had less of the anonymous power they have in cars driving down side streets and alleys. A bust in the mid-1970s drove the low end of the trade into the West End and Mount Pleasant, where vigilant and vigilante NIMBYism finally scattered the women into the Downtown Eastside, where dozens were later picked off by convicted serial killer Robert Pickton. When I spoke to Francis just after *Red Light Neon* came out, he told me, "I want to emphasize two things about the book. First of all, it's *not* about the missing women; it's a history of vice in the city, and, hopefully, enjoyable and colourful to read and so on. But the second thing is, *it is* about the missing women, because it's the background. The attempt is to provide the context, to understand what's going on now."

As for drugs, Lani Russwurm explains on the Past Tense Vancouver blog how, to a great extent, many of the problems facing the Downtown Eastside today resulted from the campaign to shut down the businesses in which drugs were being sold and consumed, so that now "derelict storefronts permeate the neighbourhood and give it its blighted appearance while users and dealers fill the streets and alleys. This is what makes the area scary for tourists and why businesses are reluctant to set up shop in the Downtown Eastside."[75]

At the top are the criminal organizations making billions of dollars. Their profits get bigger in inverse proportion to how illegal we make their product. That wealth, and the corollary firepower to protect it, has turned ad hoc groupings into permanent corporate-militia hybrids with infinite new business concerns, as happened with the American mafia during and after the prohibition of alcohol. When fortunes grow that big, social rot climbs too, helping make the economy more mercenary not only by example but also through real, transactional relationships. That kind of money doesn't float around a city's ankles, but around its neck.

My friend Dwayne is in love with the Burrard Bridge and will take it to get anywhere he needs to go. Going from Point Grey to Commercial Drive? Take the Burrard Bridge, then go up Georgia. Downtown to Granville Island? Take the bridge and then a left on 4th. Calgary to Lethbridge? Take a plane to Vancouver, take the Burrard Street Bridge, get back on the plane.

Although the bridge is breathtaking and easily the city's finest, "the grand dame [...] wearing its art deco styling elegantly, with its playful light towers at each end,"[76] Dwayne's love affair with it still seems excessive. My wife and I tease him that he lost his virginity there and drives over the bridge to recapture the moment; the story is unlikely, however, as he moved to Vancouver from back east at an age when to have only then lost one's cherry would be remembered with embarrassment rather than nostalgia. I think Dwayne's fondness for the bridge comes from its iconic place in the history of the city's peace movement, having been filled from sidewalk to sidewalk and over the length of the span by people like Dwayne (and countless others) during many of the city's marches against war and nuclear arms.

"Vancouver Loves Peace" seems like a saccharine headline (it appeared in the spiritual magazine *Common Ground* in May 2006) as well as being obvious and uncontroversial—like "Toronto Appreciates Family" or "Edmonton Is Strongly Inclined toward Warm, Friendly Handshakes." But in fairness, the city does have a strong, deep tradition of celebrating peace. The twin North Shore mountain peaks that many of us call the Lions are referred to by the Squamish nation as the Two Sisters, in honour of a pair of girls who brought an end to hostilities between the Squamish and the Haida. In 1918, Vancouver workers held the first general strike in the country's history to protest the killing of labour leader and anti-war activist Albert "Ginger" Goodwin.[77] Goodwin had presented himself two years earlier, in the thick of World War I hysteria, as a Socialist candidate for the provincial legislature on an explicitly anti-war ticket; he was killed by the RCMP in the wilds of Vancouver Island after refusing to report for duty when his health-related draft exemption was revoked.[78] The Vancouver Trades and Labour Council strike in protest of his murder was disrupted by a group of veterans gone wild: flush from the fight for democracy, they busted into the city's Labour Temple, assaulting labour activists, then making them kiss the flag.[79] Nevertheless, a city-wide, multi-industry strike had been organized and carried out around a political rather than bread-and-butter issue, and the issue was intimately bound up with questions of war and peace.

In the *Common Ground* article mentioned above, author and activist Rex Weyler does a bullet-point history of the peace movement(s) in Vancouver from the late 1960s into the early twenty-first century; Weyler, a founding member and historian of Greenpeace (a compound word whose second component seems to have been excised in the public's memory, who tends to remember the organization exclusively as an ecological movement) has an interest, obviously, in the movements of the late '60s and early '70s, which he recollects as bound up inextricably with the birth of an independent, radical Vancouver media (specifically Dan McLeod's *Georgia Straight*) and a counter-hegemonic cultural movement.[80]

But the high water mark for the Vancouver peace movement—at least in terms of numbers, broad social appeal, and support from city officials—was the mayoralty of Mike Harcourt in the mid-1980s, which saw the city council co-sponsor, with the coalition End the Arms Race (EAR), a Walk for Peace over 100,000-people strong. Even back then, some posited that the high turnouts could at least in part be attributed the apolitical, motherhood-and-apple-pie version of peace on offer;[81] others, involved in today's anti-war movement, long for the glory years and the huge crowds of the 1980s, when Vancouver was declared a nuclear-free zone, and civic referenda on disarmament could win eighty percent support from the electorate.[82]

My first anti-war marches were with EAR and the city's March for Peace and Planetary Survival—my dad took me when I was just a couple months shy of eleven years old; by this time the marches were so profoundly apolitical that, though Vancouver now had a right-wing mayor (Gordon Campbell), the city could still endorse the march, and his worship could still address the rally.[83] Over the course of the 1990s, anti-war movements would come together ad hoc around particular conflicts, often involving a relatively permanent cast of leftist and religious types opposed to war on principle working with representatives of whichever ethnic group was being targeted (though vast political differences between, say, pro-gay socialists and Chetnik chauvinists from deep inside the Serbian

Orthodox Church made the organizing against the NATO bombing of Serbia an interesting and sometimes-dramatic proposition).

After the felling of the World Trade Center and the invasion of Afghanistan, an attempt was made to put together a more permanent Vancouver coalition against war and the hysterical Islamaphobia overtaking even the supplest minds of the great, liberal West. But the result, MAWAR, the Movement Against War and Racism, didn't last long, despite producing some fairly wicked T-shirts and a decent little newsletter. It wasn't until the lead-up to the second war against Iraq that a coalition came together, beginning with the groups that had been working to lift the sanctions against Iraq as well as some church and labour organizations. Eventually named Stopwar.ca—a few of us never got over the embarrassment of the name, with its useless electronic suffix, and eventually just dropped it, referring to the coalition as simply Stopwar—the group organized the massive, nightly demonstrations downtown the week the bombing started, gaining confidence and influence quickly; for many of us on the left, it had been the first time in a long while (and for the younger ones, the first time ever) that we were articulating the opinion of the majority. Filling the streets of downtown Vancouver, seething with anger and with fear, we felt like we had momentarily broken out of the rote symbolism and metaphors of political action; we felt big in a way you never do in Vancouver—big even next to the water and the mountains. It was exhilarating.

Though we were sure we had put together something very important, over the course of the following months the coalition was very nearly torn apart by a nascent cult called the Fire This Time Movement for Social Justice (FTT), a weirdo groupuscule built around a charismatic Iranian named Ali that has since become a wild footnote in the political history of a city that has seen more than its fair share of nutty radical splinter groups. FTT had already, using a combination of race-baiting and bullying, broken apart the Anti-Poverty Committee, which had been a vibrant, radical effort leading the charge against Gordon Campbell's austerity measures and had played a leading role in squatting the Woodward's building in the Downtown Eastside. Over the course of the spring, summer, and early fall of 2003, every meeting of Stopwar.ca became a tense and nauseating ordeal, until finally, in October, the leaders of FTT were expelled—but not before they had broken into one coalition member's email account and published the stolen messages, even sending a package of them to the *Vancouver Sun* and *Province*. The meeting at which the expulsion took place, at the Maritime Labour Centre, devolved into a bizarre sit-in, followed by a cacophony of scattered screaming matches and increasingly insane assertions, like the insistence that FTT had registered the name Stopwar.ca and therefore had legal rights to it. Finally, the expelled members resigned themselves to the situation and founded Mobilization Against War and Occupation (MAWO)—and began the process of eating themselves alive. A handful have since made it out and made amends.

After the FTT/MAWO debacle, a miracle happened: any and all arguing, obstinacy, and stupidity that had been present in Stopwar ceased completely. It wasn't that FTT had had a monopoly on immaturity or sectarianism in the group before they'd left, but those of us remaining after the split felt like a married couple that had made it through a hostage situation and so weren't going to worry too much about who left the cap off the toothpaste. For me, working with Stopwar has been a high point in my political life.

The high point of the high point came on March 20, 2004, one year after the Iraq invasion and with the war still raging, when 25,000 Vancouverites poured onto Sunset Beach in protest. (The crowd filled in around the roller hockey rink, wherein the game didn't stop for a second, leading one friend to ponder later on, what would have to happen to make them stop playing?) The rally was part of a coordinated national and international day of action, but Vancouver's event was by far the biggest in the country, due in no small part to our featured speaker, Noam Chomsky. I got to emcee that rally; standing in front of tens of thousands of people, I introduced Chomsky and shook his hand while the crowd rent the air with the greatest sound I'd ever heard followed by the greatest silence—25,000 people as quiet as a painting, hanging on to Chomsky's every word. From where I was standing I could see the Burrard Bridge behind the crowd, which had taken it to get to the beach from Peace Flame Park at the edge of Kits. To be fair, that actually is the best route there.

MUNICIP
POLITICS

I own an autographed copy of the old, yellow, 230-page booklet produced for the twenty-fifth anniversary of Vancouver's left-wing civic party, COPE. The booklet is called *Working for Vancouver,* and there are two inscriptions, one from Gary Onstad, a long-time COPE pioneer and former school board trustee, and another from Larry Campbell, Liberal senator and former mayor of Vancouver. One message reads, "In Solidarity, Gary Onstad," and the other says, "All the best, Larry Campbell." The difference between the sentiments expressed, the gulf between the "in solidarity" of the left and the "all the best" of the centre, perfectly frames one of the fundamental, sometimes-creative, sometimes-destructive tensions in the municipal politics of a city with a very well-defined civic right and civic left, but where major trajectories and trends are decided by whatever's going on in the centre (plus whether people on the east side vote—the ones on the west side nearly always do).

I don't mean to suggest, by contra-distinguishing their autographs, that there was tension, creative or otherwise, between Onstad and Campbell. I've never met either man, though I do have the not-proud distinction of having been cited by Onstad in his 2006 email resigning from the COPE executive committee;[84] Onstad was referring to an online piece I'd written criticizing the then-new formation of Vision Vancouver and COPE's leadership that he'd been forwarded. He called the piece "vitriolic," which, in the cool light of day, I can admit that it was, even if many of the points made were legitimate (and anybody can seem intemperate if you isolate all the adjectives in an angry piece of writing). My only defence— besides being twenty-five at the time and not having an editor—was that the essay was written on election night 2005, after the split between COPE and the Friends of Larry Campbell (who quickly became Vision Vancouver, which some say is the largest municipal political party in the country) had resulted in the mayoralty of the inept polyglot Sam Sullivan[xiv] and a majority for the centre-right Non-Partisan Association. My emotions, like everyone else's, were running high.

For as long as Vancouver has been electing municipal governments, very rich people and their very rich friends have sought and received myriad concessions—the railways and the sugar refiners were two early beneficiaries that made things whiter and, as a result, worse for people's health—while at the same time swatting

xiv. It has always amazed me that the media, whenever it covered Sullivan's habit of picking up a new language and pledging to learn another, always covered the announcements so positively; learning a new language is *very hard* and takes a *lot* of time, and given what everyone saw as Sullivan's lackadaisical approach to governance, it surprised me that no reporter ever thought to ask whether it might not be more appropriate to wait until after he was no longer mayor of a city hosting the Olympic Games in the middle of a housing crisis to start turning himself into a living, breathing Rosetta Stone.

away attempts from the left to enact more progressive legislation. Sometimes this has worked, sometimes it hasn't. Of Louis Denison Taylor, or "L.D.," Vancouver's oftenest-serving mayor and one of the first anti-elitists to break the capitalist monopoly on civic government, historian Daniel Francis wrote: "[M]uch as he complained about the powerful elites, they were not strongly enough established to deny an outsider like himself the success that he craved," though Francis does document the left-baiting and unfair accusations of corruption and criminal ties that Taylor experienced, not to mention the hostility of the press.[85] Although he was a life-long anti-Asian racist, Taylor also brought about important advancements in Vancouver democracy such as an eight-hour day for civic workers and the vote for (white) women.[86]

When talking about the Non-Partisan Association, the preferred governing mechanism of the Vancouver establishment, people often point to the irony of a party's being named after its non-partisanship. The designation dates back to the Depression-era realization that the two big parties, the Liberals and the Conservatives, had to put aside their differences at the civic level in order to block the growing support for the socialist Co-operative Commonwealth Federation (CCF), which had elected the city's first female council member, Helena Gutteridge, and then a CCF mayor, Lyle Telford.[87] The unite-the-right-and-centre strategy was later employed on the provincial stage by a former NPA mayor, Gordon Campbell, in the BC Liberal party. In the decades after the Liberal-Conservative civic truce, there was a new reality in Vancouver, as SFU professor Donald Gutstein describes in his foreword to *Working for Vancouver:* "Each election the backroom power brokers of the Liberal and Conservative (and later Social Credit) parties would get together with the boys from BC Electric, CPR, the Vancouver Board of Trade and some of the big corporate law firms, and decide who they would run on the Non-Partisan Association slate. Their agenda was simple: keep the 'socialists' out of city hall and make the world safe for developers."[88]

Gutstein identifies this as the general trend until the year 1968, a defining one around the world, from Memphis to Prague to, apparently, Vancouver, where new municipal parties were formed by Liberals disgruntled with the arrangement in the NPA as well as the leftists surrounding socialist lawyer Harry Rankin, TEAM, and COPE.

This reality, under various permutations and with myriad variables, has defined Vancouver politics in the forty-plus years since: periods of right-wing ascendancy with the support of the centre, punctuated by periods of bumpy cooperation between the progressive elements of the centre and the left.

The high point of this cooperation was probably the mayoralty of Mike Harcourt from 1980 to 1986—the low point unfortunately followed COPE's greatest moment of triumph, its sweep of all three levels of civic government in November 2002. That year, I reluctantly put aside my suspicion of any politician formerly of the police and voted for Larry Campbell, a.k.a. "The People's Campbell." My friends and I went to the victory party at the Vancouver Public Library with a sense of political jubilation—the intoxication of the good guys having won and the squat at Woodward's going strong—and the sense that the city had become a citadel successfully resisting the siege from the province. The front foyer of the VPL central branch, in its Roman Coliseum style, was packed shoulder to shoulder that night with revellers of unimaginable happiness, who were just a few weeks away from being about as friendly as Christians and lions: At the next COPE executive committee meeting, acrimony apparently broke out immediately over Campbell's announcement that he planned to break up the Woodward's squat.

Over the next couple of years, the two factions—dubbed "COPE Classic" and "COPE Lite" by the *Georgia Straight*'s Charlie Smith— split time and again over policy issues, slot machines at the Hastings Racecourse, and the construction of a massive, Richmond-Airport-Vancouver (RAV) Line (now called the Canada Line) along Cambie Street, despite the fact that the Arbutus Corridor seemed the more logical, less invasive, more ecological option.

The differences often came down to the contradictions within the Vancouver labour movement, which vacillated between its commitments to progressive public policy on the one hand and make-work projects on the other. This contradiction is nearly as old as the city, going back at least as far as the split in the Vancouver Trades and Labour Council over the issue of Deadman's Island in 1899. While the city fought over whether the small island next to Stanley Park should be leased to an American logging concern who wanted to clear cut it, various factions in the labour council—folks normally on the same side of political struggle—devolved into a bitter war over whether working people needed more park space and protection of the natural commons, or more industry and jobs cutting down trees.[89]

It's been argued by some that the biggest problem with COPE's victory in 2002 was that the tent was too big—that the reason the relationship with Mike Harcourt stayed "shaky, but frequently successful"[90] was that at the end of each fight, everybody got to go home and sleep in their own beds. As I wrote in the *Georgia Straight* about the potential for patching things up between COPE and Vision in 2007, "[t]he evolution of Vision and COPE into distinct organizations rather than embittered factions of the same party brings to mind a dear friend of mine who after having divorced her husband, found that she was now able to get along with him swimmingly."[91] Since Vision's landslide win (on one of the lowest voter turnouts in the city's history, not normally a good thing for the left's chances) in November 2008, COPE and Vision have voted together when it's made sense, and not when it hasn't (one more-than-slightly disturbing case of the latter being when Vision wouldn't go along with a COPE motion to make VANOC respect the Charter of Rights and Freedoms). And why shouldn't that be how things are done? The attempt to build a sort of nonpartisan association on the centre-left led to an implosive acrimony that gave the city Mayor Sam Sullivan, a man whose proudest claim is the ability to say the sentence "I am an ineffective leader" in thirty-eight languages and dialects. I say "in solidarity," you say "all the best." Live and let live.

MOVING AROUND

When I used to live at the intersection of Main Street and 49th Avenue, my bus stop coming home was at the final, wheezing crest of the tired, cramped, and asthmatic Number 3 Main bus. Its analogue, the Number 3 Downtown, was by contrast a sprightly and optimistic go-getter, warmed up by the short climb from Marine Drive to my apartment like a roller coaster does on its first incline, ready to coast down the hill. But the 3 Main was frustrated and exhausted, packed and furious, and seemed to make two stops on each of the fifty blocks between the SkyTrain station and home. Because the 3 is a trolley bus line, powered by the thick, ugly cables to which it's tenuously attached by thick, ugly poles, whenever the dinosaur pulled over, the sounds of the motor running would cut out in a sad sputter, whining back to life again with great effort as it pulled back away from the curb. Somehow those sounds made it feel like we were moving even slower.

Every now and again, claustrophobia would take hold of a passenger, and that person, snapping, would decide to pick a fight with somebody else on the bus. Usually, that somebody else was me. (There's something about fat men, I think, that attracts guys who want to fight; it could be that we look big, so guys don't seem like a pussy for calling us out, or it could just be the ersatz bosoms.) I remember one in particular, pushed up in the back left corner of the bus belligerently drinking a root beer, who engaged me in eye contact then japing that very nearly brought us to fisticuffs.

A few weeks later, I was walking down Hastings Street around midnight and there he was again. Eyeing each other curiously, we simultaneously clicked on whom the other was, and why he looked so familiar. He smiled sheepishly.

"Hey man," he said, "I'm really sorry about the other day. It's just," he went on, palms upturned, "*that fucking bus.*"

Vancouver is not an easy city to get around in. In fact, it's the kind of city that you come back to after a trip to Montréal where you never had to wait more than five minutes for a bus (even in several feet of snow) that whisked you onto the quick, efficient Metro system and shake your head at in disgust while you wait to get on the 99 B-Line in a queue so long that you're actually backed up into the Commercial Drive SkyTrain station which, just like all the other stations, doesn't even have fucking turnstiles. That's right, no turnstiles; just security guards who may or may not pop on to

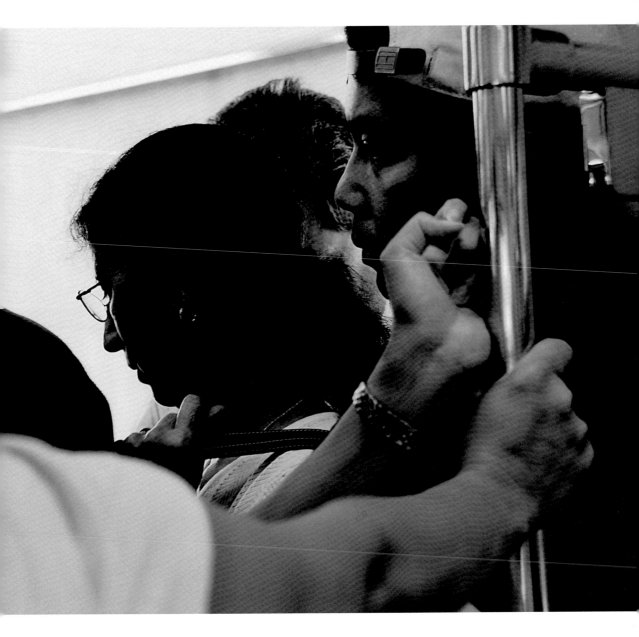

your car and ask for proof of purchase. The security on the light rail system in Canada's third largest city uses an admixture of Pollyanna honour system and Foucauldian panopticon.

Vancouverites love to brag about their decision to build a major city without highways—a forward-thinking orientation (especially given the timing of the choice, made in the late 1960s and early '70s)

that seems to indicate a level of city planning practically European in its sophistication. In their book *City Making in Paradise: Nine Decisions That Saved Vancouver*, Ken Cameron, Sean Rossiter, and former mayor Mike Harcourt count "saving Strathcona" from highways as one of their titular choices. Besides setting us on course for a more beautiful, less vehicular city, the campaign against highways was also an inspiring story of people's power, galvanizing the Chinese community especially, but also leading to a 1972 municipal election that brought defeat to the right-wing NPA for the first time since the 1930s.[92] Although the campaign was too late to save Hogan's Alley, the historic centre of Vancouver's black community, it was in every other way a huge advance for the city.

Except that the city didn't make what seems like the natural corollary decision and turn itself into an alternative transportation mecca. Ideally, a city should make it hard to own a car but easy to take buses and trains. And yet, even if people think of Vancouver as a city

I HAVE TO GET USED TO WHAT THEY CALL "HIGHWAYS" HERE IN VANCOUVER. THE "LOUGHEED HIGHWAY." ARE YOU KIDDING ME? LOOK, VANCOUVER: YOU CAN'T JUST CALL A STREET A HIGHWAY BECAUSE YOU DON'T HAVE ANY. IT'S LIKE SOMEBODY WENT TO THE MAYOR AND SAID, "WE NEED MORE HIGHWAYS," AND THE MAYOR SAID, "WELL, WE DON'T HAVE ENOUGH MONEY FOR MORE HIGHWAYS, BUT WE HAVE ENOUGH FOR MORE SIGNS. WHY DON'T WE JUST CALL BROADWAY STREET THE LOUGHEED HIGHWAY, AND MAYBE NOBODY WILL NOTICE THAT THERE'S *BUS STOPS* AND *CABS* PICKING UP PEOPLE. *ON THE HIGHWAY."*

TIM RYKERT

with no highways, nobody thinks of it as a place where you can easily live or work without a car—Vancouver is a city where it's hard to own a car, but it's even worse to have to take a lunging, fogged-up, overcrowded bus that stinks of stale rainwater and whose only advantage in traffic is that it gets the right-of-way when changing lanes.

At the turn of the twentieth century, Vancouver had a very extensive streetcar system, as well as an interurban train out to the more established city of New Westminster.[93] Built in 1890, the streetcar system was snatched up by BC Electric at the bottom of the market during the Depression just a few years later; BC Electric soon became one of the most powerful lobbies in the city. In an interview between Vancouver historians, streetcar expert Henry Ewart told Jim McGraw that in the first decades of the twentieth century, virtually every ad for real estate in the city bragged of how close the property was to the streetcar line[94]—a sharp contrast to today's attitude toward living close to the SkyTrain. The trains and, especially train stations, are thought to bring noise and unsightly construction and concrete as well as crime to neighbourhoods, and those with more money and pull will do anything to avoid them. Shit rolls downhill in cases like these, as when the super-rich folks along the ready-made Arbutus Corridor offloaded the site of the north-south Canada Line onto less-but-still-affluent Cambie, tearing up one of the city's historic commercial-residential boulevards and costing the taxpayers billions in the process.

Almost 100 years after the first streetcars ran through Vancouver, the city hosted Expo 86, a transportation-themed World's Fair (hosted by a robot named Ernie and a leprechaun named Jimmy) built around getting Vancouver a SkyTrain system that would act as a showcase for international markets.[95] More than two decades after that, when it comes to moving cars, trains, buses, feet, and bicycles, Vancouver is still running in a dozen different directions (figuratively, not literally—it's impossible to get around, remember).

In 2009 the city elected just about the bicycliest mayor that it could find, right before discovering a deep, abiding social rage against cyclists. When he was running for office, there weren't enough cameras in the world to catch all of former-juice-magnate Gregor Robertson's two-wheeled photo ops, and once he got elected, his helmet and pant-strap gave him a certain hayseed-does-good quality, like Jimmy Carter's White House solar panels. Over the course of his bids, first for the Vision Vancouver candidacy, then for the mayoralty, he appealed to cyclists as their guy. It seems he didn't even know how the SkyTrain fares worked when it was revealed that he had received, but not paid, a violation ticket from Translink security for riding multiple zones with a single-zone ticket. Robertson's cyclist-ness worked sort of like Barack Obama's blackness: the people who rode bikes could look at him and say, "He's one of us, finally!" while drivers could assuage their car guilt by voting

I WAS HAVING SEX WITH A BUS DRIVER THE OTHER DAY, AND I WAS LIKE, "BACKDOOR PLEASE! (PAUSE) THANK YOU!"

DAVE SHUMKA

200

for one of "those people." (It should be noted that Robertson's NPA opponent, Peter Ladner, was also an avid cyclist, but the meme never stuck to *him*.)

And yet somehow, just a few months into Robertson's tenure as mayor, Vancouver sunk into a sweaty, angry fit of bike panic like I've never seen before. In his book *Drive*, Tim Falconer says that "[c]ity dwellers come in three categories: drivers (and passengers), cyclists and pedestrians. Each one can't stand the other two."[96] In Vancouver in the summer of 2009, the city—which has been rife with class, race, and gender antagonisms since its inception—suddenly decided that the most important category of communal hostility was Falconer's tripartite social division. Suddenly the goddamned cyclists running four-way stops all the goddamned time became the real source of misery on Vancouver's roads, and everyone was full of stories about scofflaw peddlers. "It's like the two-minute hate," one friend said to me. Gangs of bikes had become a bigger public menace than biker gangs.

The vehicular populism reached a frenzied, fevered pitch in the lead-up to Mayor Robertson's Burrard Bridge bike lane trial (a lane for cars was redesignated for bike use only), which the media became convinced would wreak the sort of havoc on the city that Evangelicals reserve for the perverts and infidels who miss the Rapture.[xv] It was undisputed that the new bike lane would choke whole sections of the city with snaking traffic nightmares, turning the bridge and its feeder arteries into idle parking lots dumping more greenhouse gases than ever into the air, with cars and bikes pretzelling each other in a series of never-ending accidents, forcing pedestrians to run a grim, terrifying gauntlet wherein countless innocents would perish. Motorists started demanding to know how the poor little pedestrians would get around, sort of like the way Canada pretends to care about Natives whenever Québec threatens to separate.

Only nothing happened. The bike lane opened and everybody adjusted painlessly. Vancouver media almost never gets big traffic predictions right—in the lead-up to the infamous, months-long 2001 bus strike, people predicted that the city would come to a standstill; the first day, and every one thereafter, traffic patterns were perfectly normal, and the city went about its merry business while the old, young, and poor people who needed the bus did

xv. Our television show, *The Citynews List*, was no better than any other—even if I argued that the congestion was ultimately a good thing that would discourage drivers and spur them to demand better public transit, I still thought it was going to happen.

whatever walking, hitchhiking, or sitting and rotting that they had to do. But nobody ever has to apologize for getting things wrong—the huffy, right-wing columnists who predicted Armageddon in the event of a bike lane didn't have to climb down off the ledge, embarrassedly poke their glasses back up on their noses, and say, "Man, don't I feel stupid."

Instead, the bike rage kept burning, only now the target was the raucous, monthly, civilly disobedient group bike ride, Critical Mass, whose July 2009 ride took place on the hottest weekend in Vancouver's recorded history (risking fistfights and other general *Do The Right Thing*-style urban madness, not to mention the heat stroke that some might suffer in their cars).

Pro-cycle letter writers to the Vancouver newspapers the following week put things into perspective; basically, their message was that if folks didn't start listening to what the Critical Mass cyclists were on about, *every* summer weekend was going to be the hottest one on record.

And there's the rub, really. It's not just about saying "there are cyclists in the world, and pedestrians, and drivers, and they're all sort of irritated with each other, so let's figure out a way for everybody to be happy and do what they've gotta do," as though we're three siblings arguing over the remote control. A more apt analogy would be "Timmy wants to watch *Seinfeld*, Stacey wants to watch figure skating, and Petey is addicted to crack cocaine and he keeps selling off the furniture to get it even though his eyes are sinking in." In *This Magazine*, Falconer outlined a twelve-step program for fighting our addiction to cars.[97] Vancouver has made some decisions in its past that will make taking those twelve steps a little easier—but the city has a history of bad habits that, combined, can cancel out even something as monumental as rejecting highways. Habits like under-funding transit or bankrupting it with unnecessarily capital-intensive, prestige mega-projects that preclude other, more important options. In the spring of 2009, David Beers at the *Tyee* reported that for the price of the new Port Mann bridge, 200 kilometres of light rail could be built in the suburbs[98]; a few months before that, he reported that for the price of a proposed SkyTrain to UBC, taxpayers could afford to buy each first-year student a Prius, in perpetuity (imagine how much light rail we could get).[99]

Cars, bikes, feet, and public transit aren't four benign choices—
they're three fantastic ones, and one that's ruining everything.
Vancouver has stood up to it before, and could do so again. If not,
with air pollution and hotter temperatures, we could all be wheezing as heavily as the Number 3 Main.

FOOD

Over the course of my adolescence—not my life, mind you, but my teenage years—sushi went from being a punchline novelty food that appeared only in sitcom scripts to underline how essentially foreign Japan was ("Raw fish! I mean, *raw* fish!") to being a ubiquitous Vancouver meal, the rapidly proliferating purveyors of which seemed to be immune from the laws of market saturation. A lot of Vancouver's sushi restaurants are owned by Chinese and Koreans, which is in a way the greatest compliment of all, like if German food were so good that Poles and Czechs insisted on selling it. Of course, Japanese war crimes are far from most Vancouverites' minds when they eat sushi, which is how the most celebrated sushi restaurant in town can be called Tojo's. Yes, I know it's his name, but that's beside the point—I don't care how good the fettucine Alfredo is, nobody's booking dinner at Mussolini's. Nevertheless, Chef Tojo initiated the city into the ranks of sushi pioneers rather than mere imitators: legend has it that the rice-on-the-outside sushi roll was invented by Tojo because his closed-minded white patrons were grossed out by the seaweed, and so he wanted to hide it, like you would with a kid who's a picky eater. Thus, by being slightly prejudiced and as stupid as children, white Vancouver hoisted the city onto the top rung of sushi innovation; it's a real sheesh-meets-west story.

The North Americanization of another Japanese tradition, the competitive cooking program *Iron Chef*, brought another boon to the city's culinary scene: in 2005, all-star Vancouver chef Rob Feenie, formerly of Feenie's and Lumière, won Battle Crab against Iron Chef Masaharu Morimoto in a stunning, upset victory that ended with Feenie's presenting the judges with a brazen, crab-based dessert that stood in bold, ballsy contrast to Morimoto's hum drum savoury rice dish. [100] The news of Feenie's victory—and the use of his honourary title, Iron Chef Rob Feenie—burst through the wall between foodies and the public at large, and the rarefied snobs of haute cuisine, who had for years been trumpeting Vancouver's kitchens, were joined by the unwashed, Cactus-Club-eating masses in feting the city's culinary arts. (Having to some extent erased the border between high and low food in the city, Feenie was able to take advantage, after a falling-out with his business partners, of the new back-and-forth by taking a gig as something called a "Food Concept Architect" with the Cactus Club restaurant chain.) The city's chefs became celebrities to an extent that they hadn't been before; at one point, faced with the total economic collapse of Cambie Street during the construction of the Canada Line, the Shop the Line campaign featured Vikram Vij of Vij's and the neighbouring Rangoli Grill endorsing the concept of continued shopping along the boulevard.

Elite Vancouver loves to talk about how exciting fine dining here is. For starters (maybe a little soup?), everybody knows that eating and celebrating a wide range of cuisines is a great way to buy anti-racist credentials on the cheap. A Vancouver that has and enjoys great Chinese, Indian, Japanese, Thai, and even Vietnamese cuisine (though there are fewer high-rent versions of that on offer) is a city that has come to grips with its racist past and transcended it; thirty years ago, nobody but Asians and Maoists could use chopsticks, but if you met a white person from Vancouver today who hadn't mastered them you'd assume they were either in a supremacist militia or else had a palsy in their hand. Furthermore, discussion about local ingredients lets Vancouverites yammer about our very favourite subject: how lucky we are to live in such an ecologically unique and beautiful place, and don't you know you can go diving for geoduck in the afternoon and twenty minutes later go skiing on Grouse Mountain! Sure, it makes sense for a city staking a huge part of its fortunes on tourism and part-time residency to brag about its long list of fine dining options, but it also helps a city that feels insecure about its level of wealth and power vis-à-vis other cities to have mastered one of the most universal status symbols going: food.

All that helps explain the top end of the civic pantry, but then, there's always the bottom. To paraphrase the British author and filmmaker Tariq Ali, the true test of a region's cooking is its street food. Hands down, the street food most easily found and expertly produced in the city is the buck-a-slice, an economy that likely owes its existence, on both ends, to Vancouver's consumption of pot: pizza is a widely acknowledged stoner food, which at least partially explains the demand; as for the supply, though, one has to assume that the need for myriad, hard-to-follow cash businesses plays a role in keeping open at least some of these places.

That having been said, there are others whose line-ups and steady turnover would seem to indicate a success built on pizza and pizza alone—a place like Uncle Fatih's at Commercial and Broadway, for instance, where there is often a line-up into the street, must

surely be profitable on its own merits. At Uncle
Fatih's, two pieces of writing hang on the wall
that you face as you sit and eat: one is an article
from the now-defunct alternative newspaper
Terminal City, by Chris Eng, called "Ghetto Slice
Showdown," and with the (deservedly) superla-
tive review handed Uncle Fatih's, it's no wonder it's
been framed. The second piece is by a poet who has
written a piece about how the pizza there is so good
it gives him an erection.

Fatih's pizza is done in the Vancouver style,
the most salient feature of which is sesame seeds on the crust; it's
also cut smaller and sold cheaper than in other towns, where by-
the-slice pizza is sold in units similar to mall food courts. I've eaten
slices in cities all over North America, including New York; just
like Schwartz's Deli in Montréal is better than Katz's in New York,
Vancouver's pizza is better than Manhattan's.

In terms of movement eating, Vancouver is home to a large
number of vegetarians, whose list of dining-out options increases
all the time. The only one that fits the groovy 1970s California
mould is the Naam in Kits (and it ought to fit because it dates back
that far). On Main Street, hippie vegetarian is supplanted by hipster
vegetarian at the Foundation, which, though much of its menu was
convincingly disparaged to me once by someone who described it
as merely stoner food—"I'm hungry, and all I've got is black beans
and some mango"—much of it is fantastic, and they serve the city's
best nachos by a country mile. Both the Naam and the Foundation,
though, seem to indicate that the nutrients required for providing
others with good service can only be gotten from animal products.
Just up Main near 16th is the miracle that is Bo Kong, where Bud-
dhist-style vegetarian Chinese food seems to drive home the point
that being is anything but suffering, and where the textured veg-
etable protein so satisfyingly recreates a meat-like experience that
a Jewish friend I brought there had to stop eating the mock-pork
cutlets because he felt so guilty.

Vancouver is also the cradle of the 100-Mile Diet, started by two
accomplished Vancouver nonfiction writers Alisa Smith and J.B.
MacKinnon, and though the locavore inclination has been used as a
gimmick by various high-end restaurants, and the farmers' markets

around the city have become increasingly a part of the city's summer culture, the ethics of local eating is still one that's fighting its way into mainstream thinking about food. One problem, of course, is the availability and cost of local products; another is the never-ending list of *other* things to think about when buying food, and famously health-conscious Vancouver is usually trying to stay up on those. But the 100-Mile Diet is also challenged by another, competing ethic that forward-thinking people have been trying, and succeeding, to get across for decades: our internationalism of taste. Asking Vancouver to give up the foreign and sophisticated matcha tea and Pocky sticks

and mango kulfis goes against a whole range of cultivated inclinations that came at least in part from the same politically correct place as the desire to eat sustainably, which increasingly means locally (or, in starker terms, parochially). To borrow the construct employed by British ecologist George Monbiot, we have a contest between two good, decent, incompatible ethics. Similarly, Vancouver's hard-won open-mindedness about sushi is swallowing up fish stocks at a wildly unsustainable rate, leading to an increased demand for farmed fish; "lice and fish" isn't a racist joke about accents anymore so much as a scary assessment about the pests in our salmon.

See, that's why I eat pizza.

RACISM

In early 2009, two homicidal British Columbia drivers learned the legal consequences of their having each taken a life. Sukhvir Singh Khosa, a street racer who killed a pedestrian named Irene Thorpe, was deported to India in an expulsion viewed by many as the immigration board's vigilante-style revenge for the conditional sentence initially handed down by the courts. Around the same time, a young Kelowna man named David Marcel Clyne received a conditional sentence after leaving his friend's mother to die in the passenger seat of a car he'd driven off the road, his blood-alcohol levels thrice the legal limit—when he initially spoke to the police he told them in no uncertain terms, "I'm hammered."

The story of Clyne, a rural kid with a Northwest-European surname, slipped into and out of the news with barely a ripple: a Google search for his name yields eight results; the online *Province* article about his sentencing received forty-five comments. Khosa's deportation, on the other hand, was a massive triumph. The CBC website's story about his failed appeal to stay in the country garnered 354 comments including these few examples: "If I hear Khosa's been trampled by a runaway elephant, I'll start going to church"; "Let's see his future as a street racer in his shiny new Tata Nano!"; "Like most of them … they always use the 'racism card'"; and "Get out and stay out and take the rest of your family (and people) with you!" (The CBC website allows people to "agree" or "disagree" with comments. The latter comment about the "racism card" had twenty-seven disagrees and fifty-two agrees the last time I checked in June 2009.) The Khosa deportation story even ended up in the Off-Topic forum of the Vancouver Canucks website, where posters could vent along the lines of "YES! This loser should be happy, now he can street race all he wants back home in Punjab."

The difference in reaction to a story about a good ol' boy drunk driving and an Asian immigrant street racing says a lot more about BC and, especially, Vancouver than it may seem to. "Street racer" has become a code phrase in Vancouver that allows racists to lash out safely, under the pretext of condemning an obviously despicable act—it stands in for "Asian" the way "gang member" stands in for "black" in some parts of the United States, "financial speculator" stands in for "Jew" in some parts of Europe, or "terrorist" stands in for "Muslim" among respected policymakers. A friend once had an argument with a stranger about whether or not it was culturally inappropriate to use the term "rice rocket" in reference to the souped-up, imported, spoiler-bearing cars used for racing, since the *Vancouver Sun* had used the phrase. (Well, if the *Sun* says it, then surely it can't be racist!) The street racer taps directly into one of the main tropes of Vancouver's deep-running historical fear and hatred of South and East Asians: that they compromise public safety. The idea has evolved over time—they can't read the signs down in the mines; they'll hook our girls on opium and paid sex; they'll tell Tojo how to bomb us; they'll bomb our flights; they drive like maniacs; their restaurants are filthy; they turn our streets into Indy 500 tracks—but lies at the core of white Vancouver's special brand of racial paranoia.

THE ONLY RACISM I EVER EXPERIENCE HAPPENS IN MY OWN HEAD. DO YOU KNOW WHAT I'M TALKING ABOUT? IT'S THAT RACIAL SELF-CONSCIOUSNESS. EVERY VISIBLE MINORITY FEELS THIS ONCE IN A WHILE. WHITE PEOPLE FEEL IT IN CERTAIN PARTS OF RICHMOND...SURREY...THE MALL. I'M ASHAMED TO ADMIT THIS, BUT I FEEL IT WHENEVER I'M WATCHING THE LOCAL NEWS AND THEY'RE COVERING SOME STORY ABOUT A LOCAL CAR ACCIDENT TOTALLY CLOGGING UP ONE OF OUR MANY BRIDGES. AND AS THAT CAMERA STARTS TO PAN TOWARD THE DUDE WHO CAUSED THE ACCIDENT, I CAN'T HELP IT. I'M ON THE COUCH GOING, "OKAY...COME ON...NOT ASIAN...PLEASE... NOT ASIAN...NOT ASIAN...DAMN IT! CHINESE!"

PAUL BAE

Vancouver is like the United States in that it's one of the few places in the colonial-settler world where the main *cultural* racial antagonist isn't the indigenous population but another group of outsiders. In apartheid South Africa, for example, though Indians and Malaysians were subject to punitive measures and brutal discrimination, the indigenous blacks were the main targets of antipathy; in Israel, although life is harder for many Sephardim and Ethiopian Jews than it is for the Ashkenazi (so much harder, in fact, for black Jews that Israel was once briefly home to its own offshoot of the Black Panther Party), the Palestinians are always at the bottom of the heap.

Structurally, at least, that's also true in Vancouver: no one has been more ripped off or mistreated by the city than descendants of its original Musqueam and Squamish inhabitants, as well as First Nations persons from other parts of the province. The poorest, most neglected schools in the city are those that service large Native student populations. And it's impossible that Robert Pickton could have continued in his brutal endeavour for as long as he did without the general racist indifference to his victims. The 2010 Olympics cannibalizes Native imagery at the same time as it displaces rural Indians, extends recreational sporting facilities onto their traplines and unceded territory; the Games also aggravate and exacerbate a housing crisis in the city that already affects Natives disproportionately. There's no question that First Nations people have been and continue to be the main targets and victims of *structural* racism in the city.

But *cultural* racism—the raw populist nerve underlying conversation, the blubbering, inchoate rage in traffic or on transit—is a slightly different story. (I once witnessed, for example, a stammering, apoplectic old white guy tell the Sikh that he'd bumped into in the aisle of the bus, "I don't know how you do it in *your* country, but here we get out the *back* doors.") In Vancouver, over the course of its history, these kinds of sentiments have almost always been directed against East and South Asians, though that racism still occurs within the white supremacist context of settlerism. Joy Kogawa's *Obasan*, a celebrated literary treatment of Vancouver's anti-Asian racism, begins by deliberately confusing Asians and Natives in Western Canada:

> Uncle could be Chief Sitting Bull squatting here. He has the same prairie-baked skin, the deep brown furrows like dry river beds creasing his cheeks. All he needs is a feather headdress, and he would be perfect for a picture postcard—"Indian Chief from Canadian Prairie"—souvenir of Alberta, made in Japan.
>
> Some of the Native children I've had in my classes over the years could almost pass for Japanese, and vice versa.[101]

The expropriation, dislocation, and dispersal of Japanese taken from Vancouver for internment—like Joy Kogawa, like David Suzuki—is presaged by the expropriation, dislocation, and dispersal of Vancouver's original inhabitants. (Suzuki is another celebrated figure of Asian Vancouver who has gone out of his way to link himself to BC's First Nations politically, ecologically, and even aesthetically—he's nearly always photographed, for instance, wearing some sort of Haida print.) The connection is not just a literary device or rhetorical flourish; as Jean Barman has documented, many Pacific Islanders were booted out of what became Stanley Park along with the Squamish.

In Vancouver, there have historically been two categories of anti-Asian racism, and their political aims and rhetoric have occasionally overlapped: populist, working-class exclusionism (which everyone knows about and condemns), and elite, capitalist racism and its attendant exploitation. Both forms of racism are explored in author Lee Henderson's award-winning novel of pioneer Vancouver, *The Man Game*—from the rabble-rousing anti-Chinese rioting of the Knights of Labour to a pampered, mill-owner's wife who tells her Chinese houseboys not to dust before a visit from the Asian coyote who provides her husband with cheap labour. Although it has been just as pernicious as its proletarian cousin, however, elite, profit-seeking anti-Asian racism in the city has gotten far less attention than the violent, flailing rage of blue collar racists over the years. Too often, the story of Asian exclusion in Vancouver has been told as though it were simply one of working-class illiberalism in the face of capitalist cosmopolitanism and the infamous colour-blindness of the market. But certainly elite contempt for Asian immigrants, which resulted in their performing the most gruelling and dangerous labour and living in the worst and unhealthiest quarters, enacted more violence against Asian bodies than every cowboy pogrom combined.

None of which undermines the inhumanity of labour's hatred and racial violence. Like the later fascism of the British National Party (BNP) in the United Kingdom, white working-class racism in Vancouver rose out of the central contradiction of the British Empire: that despite their membership in a privileged racial caste taking stewardship over the world, proletarian Britons at the margins of the Empire were working under brutal, exploitative conditions and, on top of all that, had to compete (as they saw it) with the lower-paid members of subject races. As in the case of the BNP, a toxic stew of from-below populist self-righteousness and from-above racial supremacy became a potent organizing principle, in this case for labour and socialist individuals and organizations almost all the way along the spectrum of the left. In this context the exceptions are particularly laudable, particularly the anarcho-syndicalist Industrial Workers of the World (IWW), who maintained a principled combination of anti-racism *and* anti-capitalism. There's even an apocryphal story holding that the nickname for the IWW, the Wobblies, comes from the accented pronunciation of the letter "w" by a Chinese immigrant sympathizer.[102]

But the IWW were the exception, and the mainstream of the labour movement was animated by the same populist white supremacy that fuelled the 1907 riot, in which Vancouver racists terrorized Asian parts of the city; the riot broke up only when the residents of the Japanese quarter, joined by some of their Chinatown neighbours, armed themselves and fought back. Organized self-defence doesn't fit with the Long-Suffering Victim character of liberal, multicultural morality plays, so it too is often left out of the story—despite this, even in 1907, the targeted communities organized politically and even, in some cases, paramilitarily. Jen Sookfong Lee's dark novel of Chinese Vancouver, *The End of East*, brings to life the sometimes-spontaneous benevolent societies of the turn of the century, and the 2004 documentary *Continuous Journey* outlines the revolutionary Ghadar (Indian anti-imperialist) party and its Punjabi-language press on the West Coast.

The Ghadarites played a big role in the set piece of Vancouver's anti-Asian history, the two-month saga of the *Komagata Maru* in 1914 when 376 would-be immigrants from India were denied entry when their steamship landed in Burrard Inlet. For a white Vancouver terrified and contemptuous of the Chinese, Japanese, and "Hindoo" (as they were invariably called, though the vast majority were not Hindu but Sikh), the *Komagata Maru* incident was a triple threat: a Japanese ship and crew, leaving from Hong Kong, with hundreds of Punjabi would-be immigrants. The only way that the arrival could have been worse is if the masts of the ship had been totem poles and the Sikhs had said they were coming for a potlatch.

Like the white workers, the immigrating Sikhs had a contradictory relationship to the Empire. Though they were generally its victims, and often its opponents, their status as subjects of the King gave them certain rights in colonies like Canada, rights that took some fancy footwork on the part of Canadian lawmakers to curtail. (There's that elite racism again—and don't give me the old "the government was just bowing to the pressure of rabid labour groups" rap, a theory that, in order to make work, you have to believe that working people could get what they wanted from the government. Many of the same folks clamouring for anti-Asian legislation were also demanding workplace safety and the overhaul of the capitalist system; guess which campaigns they happened *not* to win.) One of the legal technicalities introduced to keep Indians out of Canada was the *Continuous Journey Act*, a bizarre stipulation that the boat immigrants arrived on had to come directly from the country they left, not a third port. Since there were no direct routes from India, white Vancouver was safe—until the Punjabi Sikhs who chartered the *Komagata Maru* challenged the law in 1914 by arriving at Burrard Inlet, the same body of water where Captain Vancouver met the Squamish. The ensuing two-month standoff—which ultimately resulted in the repulsion of the ship, the ejection of the would-be immigrants, and the elation of every social layer of white Vancouver—is still a blight on the city, commemorated discreetly in several places, including a replica of the boat atop the Vancouver Art Gallery. To this day, Punjabis can still find themselves the subject of racial violence. The immediate form of brute, racial beatings soared in the 1970s and early 1980s,[103] but continued into the late 1990s with the beating and murder of Nirmal Singh Gill by a group of skinheads in Surrey, and in the early twenty-first century with violent incidences in Surrey's Bear Creek Park. This racial violence also takes the form of workplace hazards in under-regulated, racialized farm labour, as in the spring 2007 school-bus crash killing several Sikh fruit pickers.[104] Sometimes, the line between random racial violence and targeted exploitation is blurred—in the heartbreaking 1981 documentary about labour organizing among Punjabi farm workers, *A Time to Rise*, a young union organizer describes a vicious beating in East Vancouver, and he is uncertain whether it was targeted intimidation by company goons, or merely a random outburst of racist violence. Of course, the two options are mutually reinforcing, and, in the end, might very well accomplish the same thing.

The same year as the *Komagata Maru* incident, a teenage houseboy named Jack Kong was found guilty of manslaughter in the death of his white, West End employer's wife, to which he had essentially pled self-defence, having brought a chair down on her as she lunged at him with a knife. His trial became a popular spectator event.[105] Ten years later, in 1924, one of Vancouver's most lurid murder mysteries began when another Chinese houseboy, Wong Foon Sing, found the body of his co-worker, a Scottish nursemaid named Janet Smith[106]—the gossipy, sensationalist fallout was like a cross between Jack Kong's earlier case and the O.J. Simpson trial. At one point, Wong Foon Sing was abducted and tortured for several weeks by men in white robes, who later turned out to have been members of elite police forces and Scottish ethnic organizations.[107]

The Asian-ness of Vancouver's social geography has always been a concern in the city, sometimes explicitly, sometimes in coded language. In the decades after World War II, the contempt for the Chinese (and black) East End, from Chinatown to Strathcona, was euphemized in the nevertheless Orwellian phrase "slum clearance," though organized community self-defence prevented the wholesale destruction of Vancouver's oldest neighbourhoods in the name of highway construction. However, the Georgia Viaduct did swallow Hogan's Alley, once the heart of black Vancouver; in this case, maybe it's appropriate that the viaduct shares a name with one of the home bases of Dixie racism.

In the 1980s and '90s, the hysteria over "Hongcouver" and billionaire developer Li Ka Shing's empire on False Creek—a tale summarized soberly by Trevor Boddy in his essay "Plastic Lion's Gate"[108]—brought the awful racial overtones of development and city planning out into the open. It also, incredibly, brought populist anti-Chinese racism in Vancouver completely full circle, as the ancillary features of anti-Chinese prejudice were the same as they had been nearly a century before: "they" can't be assimilated; "they" bring drugs into the city; "they" bring violence and gambling; "they" smell different; "they" don't sanctify normal family relationships (at the turn of the last century it was Chinese men living here as bachelors. A hundred years later, it was fathers leaving their children in Richmond while they worked in Hong Kong). Each tenet of the prejudice was recycled, reclaimed from the past, except for the one that lay at the very centre of the racists' case, which not only changed but inverted completely: in the late 1800s and early 1900s, their main complaint was that Asians were so poor, so willing to

work for and live on nothing, that no decent white man could ever
compete; in the late 1900s and early 2000s, the complaint became
that these "Hongers" were so rich, so willing to pay anything for
a house, that no decent white man could ever compete. Given that
Vancouver's white folk are the same group who came up with Continuous Journey, we don't seem to be making a lot of progress.

RESERVED FOR
IPL

HOMES

NDP politicians give up federal ridings and provincial electoral districts in East Vancouver about as enthusiastically as partygoers in Yaletown give up coke-dusted mirrors. Once you've been voted in with the social democrats on the proper side of Main Street, you've got one of the safest jobs in the city (that's part of what makes somebody like NDP MLA Libby Davies or MP Jenny Kwan so impressive; they throw themselves into constituency work even though they're about as likely to be voted out as is Kim Jong Il).

So when, after just one term in Victoria, Vancouver-Kensington MLA and former teachers' union leader David Chudnovsky threw his hands up in disgust, giving a farewell speech in which he called the provincial legislature a "sideshow" and vacating a seat that he was all-but-guaranteed to win, it was surprising. Until, of course, he reminded everyone that for "most of the last two years [he] was the critic for homelessness and mental health issues," which in BC, and in Vancouver specifically, is the kind of job that would make even an aquaphobic anorexic want to draw a bath and make some toast.

There's likely not a single issue in the city of Vancouver more widely discussed than where people live, in what, and for how much, from the very poorest (seen as an obstacle to both their own and others' happiness and well-being) to the very richest, whose real estate wheelings and dealings—along with the degree of market-scarcity introduced by the geographic enclosure of the city—helped create some of the highest real estate and housing costs in North America in the middle of a continent-wide housing boom. So yes, people in Vancouver talk about housing, sort of like the way people in Detroit used to talk about cars. The thing is, pandemic homelessness and the expulsion of the middle classes from the ranks of prospective Vancouver property owners have led some people in Vancouver to talk about real estate the way people in Detroit talk about cars *today*.

In a blog post about the city government's long history of wrangling with squatters—"[h]istorically, this has included everything from the hobo jungles of the 1930s to caves near Siwash Rock in Stanley Park"—Vancouver historian Lani Russwurm points out that though "Vancouver has always had a shortage of affordable housing [...] only in recent years has this translated into considerable numbers of homeless people forced to sleep in alleys, on sidewalks, and in whatever nook or cranny they can find throughout the city."[109]

Since the late 1990s, the problem of homelessness in Vancouver has gone stratospheric, with even conservative media, such as the *Province,* admitting that the numbers are "stunning" when it reported on a 373 percent increase in homeless over six years, starting in 2002; the article put the number of homeless in 2008 at close to 3,000 people.[110] The crisis of homelessness and the ubiquity of pan-

handling are still recent enough phenomena—beginning in earnest under federal finance minister Paul Martin's budget balancing during the 1990s—that no generation of adults yet thinks it's normal, but one is fast approaching that will reach voting age without ever having known a city where every urban block didn't have a dozen people sleeping on church steps and begging for change.

A cultural apartheid tailored to the city—a set of shared social norms and practices that puts a qualitative break between them and us—has cropped up in Vancouver as a means of making the situation understandable. It's clear to me from the way comedy audiences in the city react to a wide range of material about homelessness (it's impossible that the subject wouldn't come up again and again, the same way your doctor would eventually bring up the axe wound across your stomach if you kept haemorrhaging blood on to her floor) that, in general, we vacillate between a sort of formal sympathy on the one hand and a mean-spirited need, on the other, to imagine that these people are, in fact, a profoundly different species from us and that their situation, however tragic, is fundamentally unrelatable, and unrelated, to ours. This lets us off the hook a little bit and means that we can start thinking of the homeless as a culturally, if not genetically, distinct group, fundamentally irrational and therefore no longer subject to the normal rules—as a nod to Giorgio Agamben, you could call them "hobo *sacer*."

Here's an example of what I mean: I used to live next door to a run-down old house in East Vancouver that was being squatted by a group of homeless youth. The owner of the home had been loudly complaining to my downstairs neighbours that he was having a hell of a time getting demolition papers from the city so that he could build a nice new home (several had gone up on the block while I was living there), and now, on top of it all, he was dealing with squatters.

One afternoon, on my way home through the alley that we shared with the squatted house, I noticed smoke billowing out of its carport. I rushed in with a bucket of water and found a sagebrush smouldering on a wooden plank right above a propane tank surrounded with old papers. I phoned the fire department, who arrived quickly—along with the police—and soaked the area. The cops and the fire fighters assumed immediately that the squatters had carelessly left the hazard there; when I explained that I'd heard the landlord had been bemoaning his troubles getting demolition orders for the house, that the way the fire was set up suggested it might at least be worth looking into the possibility of a firebug, that the squatters—with whom we had never had any problems—were living there and had no interest in seeing it blown sky high, I was casually told that people like them do crazy, inexplicable things. And that was all they felt they needed to say.

RESIDENCESATGEORGIA.COM
NCOUVER
ST, SUITE 100
GEORGIA.COM
THE PRIVATE RESIDENCE
LUTHERAN URBAN MISSION SOCIETY
LUMS
THE POOR AND HOMELESS
OUR SIN AND CHALLENGE
HOMES
FOR AL
THIS

I once asked a friend, who used to be a United Church pastor before losing his faith, if he didn't think that there must be some cumulative effect on our psychologies, or our souls, passing by so many people in such dire need every day. Even generous Vancouverites who hand out a couple of loonies or toonies as they walk along a downtown street will eventually have to stop unless they're carry-

ing a piggy bank. But once your change is gone, the guy you have to apologize to has no way of knowing that you just helped out the girl up the block, so all you can do is look him in the eye earnestly and shake your head no.

The first few times, it breaks your heart, but you learn to sublimate the feeling as time goes on, otherwise you'd never leave your bed. You can feel the callous start to form, the roughening up that keeps you from having to confront the profound misery of the situation. My friend—who had once been sitting on a bench in Tinseltown mall, loitering identically to the street person at the other end of it, and had confronted the security guard who "moved along" only the homeless man—explained to me that one of his final sermons had been on the subject of our spiritual coarsening in the face of others' suffering. The church community's unwillingness or inability to be Christ-like in its response had contributed greatly to his crisis of faith.

That having been said, the wilting of my friend's and my precious sensibilities, tragic though it may be, is the least important effect of Vancouver's housing crisis, whose primary victims aren't living through an interesting quandary of moral philosophy but a real-life, physical emergency. People are dying from exposure, from burning to death in fires built to fight off the cold, from drugs that quickly become the only thing that, as comedian Rob Pue puts it, "takes the edge off of sleeping on concrete every night." Pue's bit is a response to the tongue-cluckers who tell him that giving money to panhandlers just goes to buying booze and drugs—"I didn't think my shitty little toonie was going to lead to some entrepreneurial epiphany: 'I'm going to open a savings account!'" Besides, Pue explains, if this guy knows where he can get drunk and high for two bucks, "I'm following him." It's one of the few jokes about homelessness in the city built around identifying *with* rather than *against*, and as a result, it's one of my favourites.

The same quality is also one of the reasons why Chudnovsky's resignation is one of my favourites ever delivered by a politician. After acknowledging the work of committed activists like "Jean Swanson, a true British Columbia hero; Wendy Peterson; that extraordinary advocate, David Eby; and my dear, dear friend Linda Shuto," Chudnovsky continued: "More important, I want to thank the hundreds of homeless people it was my privilege to meet and learn from over the last two years. There's more good sense and public policy expertise in any emergency shelter or on the street among those who we, to our shame, have ignored than there is on the entire government front bench."[111]

Now, maybe if the government had to *sleep* under that bench, we might get somewhere.

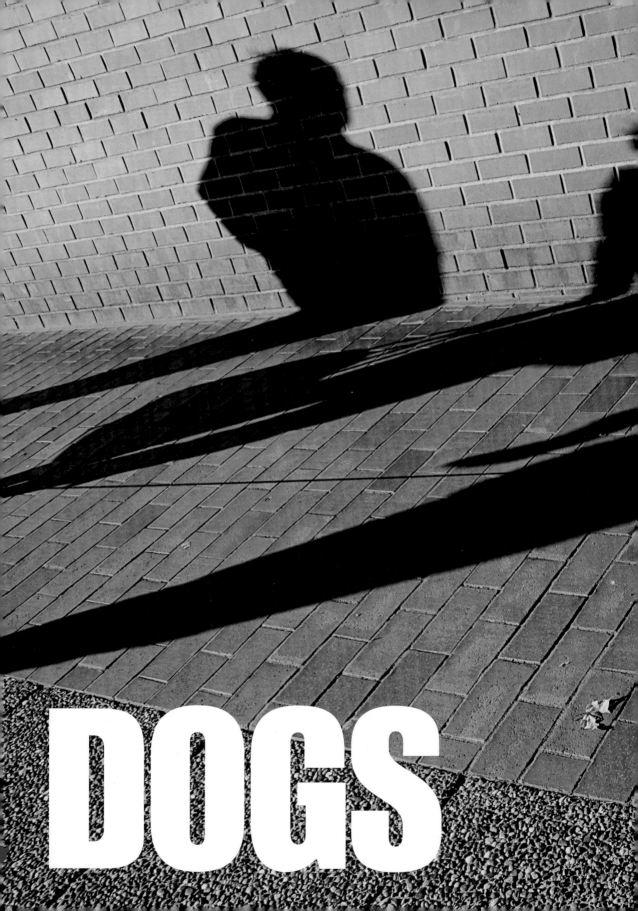

DOGS

Vancouver has very few cultural inclinations that transcend all class divisions; in fact, I can only really think of three: pot, a casual interest in the Canucks that becomes rabid in the post-season (instant fandom: just add playoffs), and dogs. The irony is that, though a love of dogs is present in every socioeconomic layer of Vancouver, from street kid to hi-tech millionaire, the specific manner in which dogs are enjoyed has become one of the prime cultural signifiers of class in the city. The street newspaper *Megaphone* once dedicated a whole issue to the subject of pets and their importance to the under-housed, citing everything from companionship to security (and, in that sense, going some ways toward answering Norm Macdonald's cheeky joke about the reaction of the dog to its homeless master: "You know I could do this by myself, right? I mean, thanks for the bandana and all…").

Conversely, any conversation about Yaletown moves quickly from yuppies to puppies: the tiny, yapping dogs so closely identified with the neighbourhood have become emblematic of its emasculated affluence. Now look, I'm not one to defend rich people, but be reasonable—they're living in twelve square feet of penthouse luxury, and you want them to keep what, a bull mastiff? Those tiny little canines—or "pocket rats," as some have called them—are, at the end of the day, the only humane choice, given the strictures of Yaletown

living. It may be one of the few instances in history of a large group of rich people showing any kind of consistent compassion.

But beyond the choice of dog size, there is doggy pampering, which is admittedly absurd, and an embarrassment to every Vancouverite not partaking in it. My dear friend and TV co-host Graham Clark has a bit about watching a typical Vancouver dog owner fill a dog bowl with bottled water. "Oh, Perrier—thank you," says the grateful pooch. "Something to wash down the taste of my own ass."

A few years ago I was assigned to write the entry on dog culture in a tourist book about Vancouver; as part of my research, I visited a little strip along 4th Avenue in Kits—once called Rainbow Road, and the mecca of hippie counterculture—where doggy luxury now reigned supreme. On the north side of the street sat an accessory shop filled with expensive dog toothbrushes and designer coats and harnesses that wouldn't have seemed out of place in one of the sex shops on downtown Granville Street, only in this case, the relationships the harnesses were meant for were built around love and long-term commitment. Directly across the road was Three Dog Bakery (I assume the name is an allusion to Three Dog Night, though I don't see how or why). Inside, there was a freshly baked selection of gourmet dog treats, each of which looked more like a wholesome, homemade cake or cookie than anything made by Mr Christie.

John Murphy, a very talented Vancouver playwright and performer, does a wonderful piece in which he plays an angry, sardonic homeless man inside just such a doggy bakery. The unsubtle thesis, obviously, is that we're letting our fellow humans languish and starve while spoiling dogs rotten; the finer, more delicate point that he captures is the porous border between cynical, embittered Vancouver and naïve, optimistic Vancouver. At one point in the monologue, the trenchcoated homeless man sidles up alongside of one of the patrons in the bakery. She's been taken aback by a counterperson asking if she'd like a personal birthday greeting for her dog written in doggy-edible icing on his cookie. "What's the matter," growls the street person, "can't your dog *read*?" Even though she's only hinted at, the audience can see the woman struggle between embarrassedly identifying with the man's gruff (but totally reasonable) sarcasm, or else throwing herself whole-hog into the experience of spoiling her pet and thus joining the happy leagues of affluent dog owners enjoying their lives double time, in human and in dog years simultaneously.

There are two ways to look at Vancouver's yuppy-puppy phenomenon as it sits next to the social cruelty of the Downtown Eastside. Being generous, we could say that under a set of circumstances where homelessness and alienation and atomization seem so big, one little dog to take care of is a realistically sized vessel for love and altruism. Less kindly, we could recall Dr Jennifer Melfi, Tony Soprano's psychiatrist on HBO's mob drama, reading with panic an essay in a psychiatric journal about the ways in which sociopaths employ a bathetic sympathy for animals, as her Mafioso patient did over the course of the series with ducks, a horse, and even a little dog, to mask their lack of empathy for the people they destroy.

Either way, I'm comforted by the fact that Vancouver's street people tend to have big, tough, hungry mutts, while the rich have tiny, shaking inbred things not used to walking on concrete. If it ever really came down it, there'd be no contest.

Please leash and clean up after your dog

BYLAW 7528

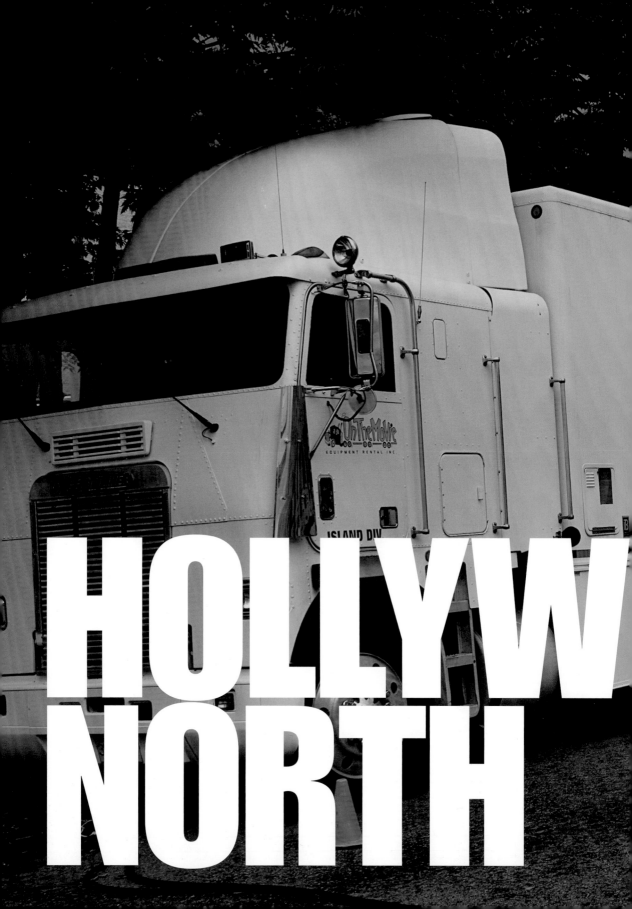

When my wife Cara and I first started dating, I didn't have any money, and so for dates I would often bring her with me to the plays and movies that I was reviewing for the *Westender* (for those of you wondering why she stuck around, she has very low self-esteem). One night Cara accompanied me to a screening, downtown on Burrard Street, of a terrible, terrible film called *Catch and Release*, starring Jennifer Garner and Kevin Smith, set in Colorado but filmed largely in Vancouver. After the picture, a nervous, young representative for the production company—a good-looking Asian kid who had been chatting with as many members of the preview audience as he could—approached us to ask what we thought of the film. I politely demurred, explaining that I was media. Cara, though, was feeling acidic.

"What have other people been saying?" she asked calmly.

"Oh, you know," replied the rep. "Cute, sort of a fun little movie."

"Has anybody said *appalling*?" she asked.

"No."

"That's what *I'd* like to say."

On the Internet Movie Database (imdb) website page for *Catch and Release,* under the heading "Fun Stuff," there is a link to a list of the film's goofs, including a handful of continuity errors and one mistake classified under "Errors in geography: There are too many plants in the town that do not grow in Colorado. Boulder has a high, cold, and dry climate, which cannot support the diversity of plants in the town."[112] The problem for imdb was that too many of Vancouver's indigenous flora were visible in the picture. (There were some architectural giveaways, too; in particular Kitsilano's characteristically colourful bungalows, set into lush, tree-filled yards as though they were cabins.) My problem, leaving the film, was that none of Vancouver's indigenous *talent* could be seen. I thought of the brilliant Vancouver writers and directors I knew, who would never be able to afford the world-class Vancouver crews wasted on American stinkbombs like *Catch and Release*, or the talented local actors subsidizing their work on Vancouver stages with bit parts for disposable TV and film—for every one Hiro Kanagawa who steals a scene in a wonderful picture like *Best in Show* (Kanagawa played the disarmingly placid pet store owner going through colour combinations on dog toys with Parker Posey), fifty more have to sell Persian rugs in a jerry-rigged bazaar to a kid on *Breaker High*, the show about a high school on a boat.

During the 1980s and 1990s, film and TV production were always a part of the scenery. In his essay "The Grid: Living in Hollywood North,"[113] writer/performer Stephen E. Miller lays out the policy, industry, and infrastructure decisions that laid the groundwork for the Vancouver film and TV phenomenon in the late 1970s—the essay is anything but a dry summary of tax regulations, but those are most stunning to me because for someone of my generation, it's difficult to think of Hollywood North as something that was consciously brought about rather than something that was always there. To my generation, Hollywood North was always sold with the same clichéd appeal to the city's topography, the standard-issue, board-of-tourism stock line: You can be in the forest in the morning, on the ski hill in the afternoon, and on the beach in the evening, (why is it that every visitor to Vancouver is presumed to have attention deficit disorder?) was retrofitted to explain why the city was a natural for the movie industry. But instead of going to these places, it was now about filming them. The explanation made sense as a kid, but looking back it seems strange if the combination of beach, forest, and mountaintop is so rare, then why would so many movies, none of them set in Vancouver, require all three? Any lingering feeling that it was the city's nature, rather than politics and economics, that kept the work coming was put to rest in 2007–08 when the Hollywood writers' strike coincided with a bloated Canadian petrodollar, leaving some terrified that Vancouver's status—what Douglas Coupland called "backlot North"—was gone for good. Many actor friends of mine went months without anything—and I mean without *auditions*, let alone work.

When I was nine, I took a summer camp drama course that was taught by a tall, thin man with a moustache who I'm almost positive was Jackson Davies, most famous for playing Constable John Constable on CBC's *The Beachcombers*. (If like me, you were just *barely* too young to have watched this long-running show, you will forever feel slightly disoriented in conversations about pop culture in Vancouver.) My parents also let me take part in an after-school snake-handling course (that sounds like a euphemism for being molested, but it isn't) with the guy who provided the snakes for at least one episode of the show. In between handing us reptiles during one of the sessions, he showed us a clip of MacGyver walking through a pit of snakes (actually, it was our instructor's foot in MacGyver's boot) before explaining to us that his name wasn't in the end credits because he got paid more money that way. I distinctly remember being as fascinated by that fact as I was by the cobra he had in a jar in a cooler (a few years later that man died after he was bit by one of his snakes).

In junior high my drama teacher was an actor—and as wonderful a teacher as he was, if you ever forgot he was an actor *first*, he'd be sure to remind you; we spent at least one class *watching his reel*. His resumé introduced me to the broad contours of an actor's curriculum vitae in Vancouver, if they've been in it from the beginning: it starts with something from *Rambo* or *The Beachcombers,* then *21 Jump Street, MacGyver, Highlander, Danger Bay, Neon Rider, The X-Files, Da Vinci's Inquest, Best in Show, Scooby Doo 2, Stargate SG-1, Battlestar Galactica*, and *Smallville,* give or take a few dozen roles for TV shows with short runs (*Pure Luck, Da Vinci's City Hall, jPod*) and a healthy dose of usually forgettable Yankee movies. When you consider how good the few programs set in Vancouver as Vancouver manage to be—like *Da Vinci's Inquest,* which looked at neighbourhood atrophy and urban policy planning through the lens of a police procedural years before *The Wire* did it on HBO—it's sad to think how infrequently it happens.

In his essay, Miller is pessimistic about Vancouver's chances at injecting more local flavour into the product: "Cancon [government mandated Canadian content] simply doesn't work. It's all a matter of the marketplace, which virtually forces Canadian film and television production into its too-familiar generic straitjacket."[114] He goes on to outline a convincingly bleak case. Still, it seems to me that the lion's share of Cancon (let alone Vancon) efforts have been aimed at boosting supply, with little work done on increasing demand. There are multi-screen theatres all over Vancouver—Tinseltown, Scotiabank, Fifth Avenue, as well as Cineplex hyper-theatres all over the suburbs—that should be regulated to showcase Canadian product just as tightly as Canadian radio stations have been, resulting in a renaissance of Canadian pop, rap, and indie-rock.

Watching Douglas Coupland's 2006 city-state comedy *Everything's Gone Green* in a Vancouver theatre was a surreal pleasure (even if the protagonist's opening montage bike ride to work made no geographical sense and was clearly about showing off the city's beauty marks to people from elsewhere). It wasn't a Great Film, but it was very good, and familiar, not to mention cathartic to see actors I knew in undisguised neighbourhoods that I frequent, talking about grow ops and downtown condos and Vancouver being dressed up like other cities for the movies.

Finally, there is one last way for Vancouver to make its mark. In the summer of 2009, popular American movie blog Film-Drunk isolated a two-second clip from the trailer to the Z-list, filmed-in-Vancouver movie *MVP: Most Vertical Primate*, about a sports-playing chimpanzee; in the isolated clip was a young man hilariously double-pumping his fists, cheering for the monkey, making a mockery of the whole movie with his ridiculous over-enthusiasm. The blogger wondered who the actor delivering "the best two-second performance in all of cinema" was. I wrote him an email because I knew: a brilliant, alternative stand-up comedian named Aubrey Tennant, who was a fixture of Vancouver's comedy scene for years (he's also the guy in the BC Lotto commercial jumping up and down in slow motion with another guy, whose toupee is flying off). For years, Aubrey had been stirring up shit as an extra on terrible films, including enraging the director of a Sean William Scott vehicle with his background shenanigans. The Film-Drunk blog followed up on the story and interviewed Aubrey, and the persona in which he answered had a very non-Vancouver take on a familiar Vancouver resumé:

> I did as much extra work as possible and stole as many scenes as I could. A few movies where I have other 2-second roles include: *40 Days and 40 Nights,* starring me and Josh Hartnett, *Stark Raving Mad* starring me and Sean William Scott [sic], *Scary Movie* starring me and Anna Faris, and *Anti-Trust* starring me and Ryan Philippe [sic], just to name a few. The TV shows in which you can see me for two seconds include several episodes of *Stargate SG-1*, starring me and Macgyver, *Higher Ground,* starring me and Hayden Christiansen [sic]—my 2-second role in that is of a gay man touching the butt of another gay man—and *Smallville,* starring me and some no namers.[115]

SPORTS

Before you read this essay about sports in Vancouver, you should know the following: although both my brother and my father are gay men in happy, same-sex marriages, my dad considers me to be the faggiest member of the family. As proof of this deficit in masculinity, I generally possess minimal interest in team sports because during the formative childhood years during which a love of competitive athletics is supposed to develop, I was the fat kid, which meant that I always had to be two things: funny and goalie. In short, I'm the kind of guy who, in a conversation about how rough and wild a hockey player Tiger Williams was, will say, "Yes, and did you know that he's not just black, but also part Asian?" Nevertheless, it seems wrong to write a book on Vancouver without talking about sports at all, so here is a franchise-by-franchise series of observations and anecdotes. If you notice that I tend to move quickly away from the specifics of the game in favour of broader, social discussions, that's called playing the zone, asshole.

THE CANUCKS

When I was a little kid, one of the only ways that you could tell that I was French Canadian was by looking at my Expos and Montréal Canadiens paraphernalia. Because our family wasn't interested in sports, if my dad could tell me today, without consulting the Internet or an almanac, what sport a power forward plays, I would take over the payments for his house (actually not as ballsy as it sounds; he lives in the Maritimes). Our loyalties to Montréal franchises were pure signifiers of ethnic identity, bolstered by the fact that the Habs were coached by someone who shared our family name. When I was about seven years old, my aunt and her boyfriend took me to watch the Vancouver Canucks play the Habs at the Pacific Coliseum where, unlike GM Place, you felt like you were at a hockey game, could feel the cold air off the ice all the way into the stands. I insisted on wearing my Montréal jersey to the game, and my aunt was convinced that we were going to be assaulted.

When we got there, at least two-thirds of the crowd was, like me, in Montréal's red, white, and blue; my aunt's boyfriend even bought me a Habs pennant. (Doesn't it seem *strange* that you could buy an opposing team's pennant at our arena?) Contrary to what revisionist Canucks fans will tell you about Vancouver being a committed hockey town for decades—fans love to wear the old, throw-back hats and T-shirts and jerseys, with the stick-in-rink *C*

and Johnny Canuck; almost all of this merchandise printed in the last couple of years—that's how it was in Vancouver until the 1994 finals, when the city got a hockey riot and some real fans (though I've had to remind ostensibly committed fans that the Canucks have been to the finals twice, once in '82).

As to the charge often levelled against Canucks fans that they're fair-weather types, consider the following: there is a comedian in Vancouver (I won't name him here and get him in trouble) who swiped a sign from a Canadian Tire that he likes to bring out every year during the playoffs. The sign reads, "No Returns on Canucks Flags." Similarly, on Citytv, my colleagues and I once did a remote segment on the *CityNews List* in which we went out into the street and asked Vancouverites to join us inside the Canucks bandwagon (a little wagon we'd found in the station's carpentry department) and chant with us a traditional Vancouver cheer: Canucks until we lose! A huge number of passers-by indulged us—I'd say a much higher percentage than normally does on streeter segments. I hosted the segment wearing a Montréal jersey with the Vancouver logo duct taped over the middle. One person was offended by it and voiced his displeasure; he was a Habs fan.

All that having been said, I'm fairly certain that I pulled for Montréal for as long as I did to cover up the fact that I had no interest in hockey. By my late twenties, when the game finally began to exert some kind of inevitable, Canadian pull on my attention, I found that I cared more what happened to Vancouver whose fans I watched the games with, whose neighbourhoods either honked in euphoria or rioted in melancholy in the event of a win or a loss, than to Montréal. For the last little while, I'd say I'm a casual fan of the Canucks, which puts me in league amongst the most die-hard supporters in the city.

THE LIONS

It's not for nothing that it's the *Vancouver* Canucks hockey team but the *BC* Lions football club; support for the CFL squad is, these days, almost completely confined to the suburbs, which at the very least seems to indicate that watery commitment to the Canucks isn't about them never having won a championship (the Lions have five Grey Cups).

When I was little, our family friend John Pankratz—who played eight seasons with the Lions, including the championship

year in 1985, and whose cabin on Galiano Island, incidentally, was the site of my proposal to my wife—would occasionally give us his alumni-section tickets to the games. My grandmother would take me, and we would sit with all the old players, and they would try to flirt with my grandmother through me by saying things like, "Son, I'll give you a dollar if your mom [*priceless!*] can tell me who led the team in touchdowns in 1961." We had a lot of fun, and for the first time I ate hot dogs measured in feet (processed meat was always a part of my CFL experience; my mom used to buy a football-shaped salami around Grey Cup time every year).

I was at the game in 1990 when the legendary Lui Passaglia broke the scoring record, and the game stopped so that the moment could be commemorated and everyone could celebrate, as they did, by yelling "Loooouuuuuuuuuu," which was baffling to me, as a ten-year-old, because I thought they were booing him (years later, my wife thought the same thing when, during a play-off shutout against the St Louis Blues in 2009, goalie Roberto Luongo was cheered the same way).

THE WHITECAPS

One time, at the airport, my family was standing in line at the check-in behind former Whitecaps player and current president Bob Lenarduzzi, his wife, and his kids. The whole family was wearing track suits.

THE GRIZZLIES

The New Orleans Jazz staying the "Jazz" despite moving to Utah is pretty much the only case of a recently moved team's name being more incongruous than the Memphis Grizzles. The Grizzlies was the name chosen by Vancouver's short-lived NBA franchise after they told my friend and co-host Paul Bae and his brother Martin—whose name-and-design idea for the team, the Vancouver Axemen, was one of the finalists—that their idea was too violent. Apparently, an animal designed by billions of years of evolution to be one of the fiercest, most efficient killers on land was a more benign choice than the woodworkers who built our province's economy. Could have been worse, though; apparently, the team was very nearly called the Mounties,[116] another species known for its often-lethal, violent outbursts, though admittedly this was before the widespread use of Tasers.

In 1995, the Grizzlies infamously saddled themselves with Bryant "Big Country" Reeves, a slow, massive, bumpkin centre prone to gaining mounds of catfish weight during the off-season. I'm convinced that Reeves' race had to have something to do with the draft pick—somebody figured that if you were bringing a black-dominated sport to a city with relatively few black people, you needed to build the franchise around a white player—but Big Country did have a great Final Four as a college player, and so there was no reason to expect he'd be as terrible as he was (watching Reeve's slow, jaunty middle-aged jog up the court, always five or ten paces behind his harder working teammates, was excruciating).

Reeves is the draft-pick sin of commission in anybody's expla-nation of why there's no longer a basketball team here; the sin of omission is passing up Steve Nash the following year. Nash, from Victoria, not only wanted to play for Vancouver (a condition that was exceedingly rare amongst professional basketball players), but he became one of the best players in the league, winning MVP two years in a row and becoming famous for a Gretzky-like style of play heavy on passing; what's more, because he's from BC, white people from Vancouver don't feel racist cheering for him. In retrospect, many argue, drafting Nash in 1996 could have saved the team.

The claim *feels* true, and sounds right, but probably isn't. People talk about the Grizzlies' draft picks as though the team selected Reeves over Nash. The Grizzlies' pick in 1996, over Nash, was Shareef Abdur-Rahim, a talented, hard-working, and pleasant player who not only made just as valiant an effort as Nash would have, but who also charmed Vancouver's Sunni Muslim community, of which he became a part. (Nash, too, made some fans in this constituency when he came out against the Iraq War, despite the fact that he was a Canadian playing for Dallas.)

The Grizzlies were a poorly managed team, but rather than reliving the draft of '96, Vancouver basketball fans should hope that between Nash's popularity and leadership skills and the light at the end of his career as a player, coupled with the small-but-growing coterie of Chinese players and the hundreds of millions of dollars that Vancouver has sunk into making itself a sports city for the Olympics, might combine to give the city a second shot. There are plenty more lethal names with local resonance to choose from; we could call them the Bikers, or the Vancouver Drunks-on-the-Sea-to-Sky-Highway. There's no *way* they could have kept that name in Memphis.

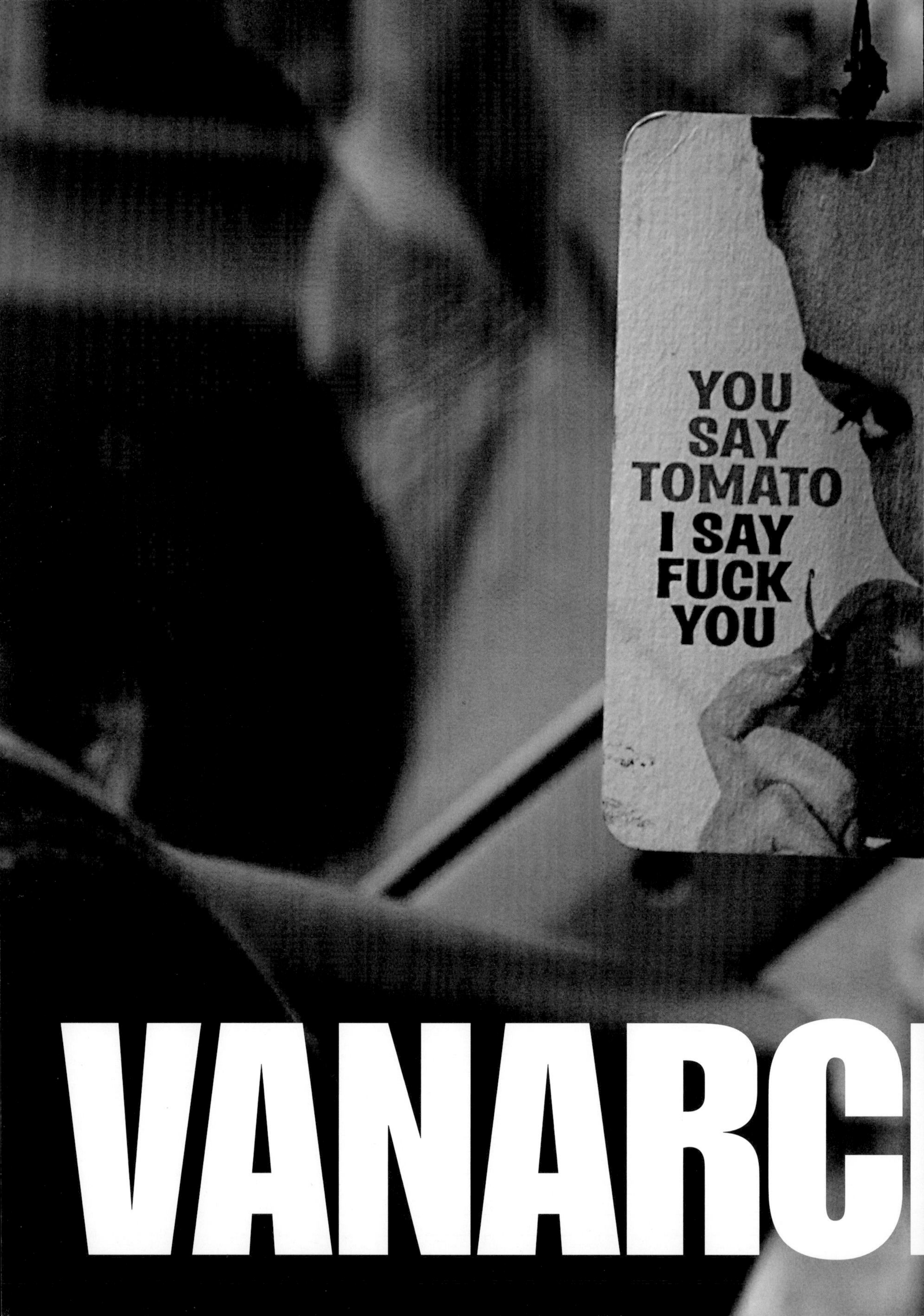

VANARC

"We had read most of the anarchist classics, of course, but, in the Vancouver style, we didn't bother ourselves too much with fine distinctions."

—Bob Sarti on the founding of the Vancouver-based anarchist journal *Open Road*, sometimes called "the *Rolling Stone* of anarchism."[117]

The conventional wisdom about punk rock is that it was, at least in part, the cynical, more world-weary response to the call of doe-eyed, optimistic hippie psychedelia. It's a slightly disheartening commentary on just how far gone into cynicism my generation is, then, that for us punk is sometimes too earnest. During my years at the SFU student newspaper, I once watched two merciless, giggling editors use mathematics to subvert the famous phrase "Talk minus action equals zero," made popular by Vancouver's hardcore punk pioneers D.O.A. Expressed as the algebraic equation $x - y = 0$, they gleefully pointed out that the formula actually reduced to $x = y$, or, in other words, talk equals action, the exact sentiment that the anarchist activists in D.O.A. were setting out to disrupt. (Before you get too worried about these two cynics, rest assured that they came out okay: one turned his economics and business degrees to the task of sniffing out fraud in Albertan financial institutions, the other ended up writing for *Adbusters* and the *Tyee*; to quote a decadent arena-rock glam sissy, "the kids are alright.")

As a political radical, and someone who likes to think he has good taste in music, I'm more than a little embarrassed to admit that the most I've ever been moved by a D.O.A. song was with an acoustic, solo version of "You Won't Stand Alone" performed by front man Joey "Shithead" Keithley on *The Mike Bullard Show* (Keithley was on to promote his autobiography, *I, Shithead*, the title of which Bullard hilariously got around by repeatedly referring to as "I, *Shih-theed*"). Admitting that your favourite rendition of a D.O.A. song is the mellow, acoustic one you heard on a chat show is sort of like saying that your favourite version of "Layla" is the one on *Eric Clapton: Unplugged*. My Uncle Phil, once a dedicated Clapton fan, was enraged by the unplugged "Layla," which he considered "lounge lizard music." The laid-back, jolly serenity missed the wrenching, inchoate agony that had been the whole point of the original.

As a variation on a similar theme, what I had liked so much about Keithley's acoustic performance was that it sounded pretty, which is to completely miss the point of D.O.A., whose visceral, jagged, political rage used the kinetic energy of hardcore punk rock to inspire a longer-lasting, potential energy engaged in various political processes. "I guess [... i]f anything I'm an example of how anger and dissent can be used as a powerful yet peaceful force," Shithead once admitted.[118] That said, Vancouver's late 1970s/early 1980s hardcore milieu also inspired plenty of political kinesis, too, culminating in the arrest and imprisonment of Gerry "Useless" Hannah, the bassist for the Subhumans, for his role in the violent acts of sabotage carried out by the Squamish Five (a.k.a. the Vancouver Five, a.k.a. Direct Action, a.k.a. the Wimmin's Fire Brigade), which included destroying a BC Hydro substation (suspected by some to be the precursor to nuclear power in BC or Alberta), exploding a van outside a cruise missile plant in Ontario (which helped lose the company, Litton Systems, its contract), and burning several Red Hot Video porn stores to the ground.

The First Book of Canadian Anarchism is Michael Ondaatje's *In the Skin of a Lion*, a novel intimately bound up with the birth of the city of Toronto. This seems unfair, on the surface, because undoubtedly the First City of Canadian Anarchism is Vancouver (that sort of hierarchical ranking runs counter to the spirit of anarchism, but we love lists in Vancouver because we're usually at the top of them). Just like the rest of the country, Vancouver has a long history of social democratic and socialist and even communist organizers and agitators; but anarchism's brand of left libertarianism, the simultaneous hostility to both state and corporate power, goes back a long time in this city and, remarkably, never really goes away.

For instance, it may surprise some people to learn that the book considered to be the "finest work [...] in the English language" about the nineteenth-century anarchist philosopher Mikhail Bakunin—who was Russian and did much of his writing in French—is one written by Mark Leier, who was born and raised in the Lower Mainland and now lives on the North Shore and teaches Canadian history at Simon Fraser University in Burnaby. I met Mark, now a dear friend, at SFU, where he peppers his lectures on BC labour history with full-voiced, banjo-accompanied renditions of old anarcho-syndicalist folk songs, including the classic "Where the Fraser River Flows":

> Where the Fraser River flows, each fellow worker knows
> They have bullied and oppressed us, but still our union grows;
> And we're going to find a way, boys, for shorter hours and
>   better pay, boys,
> We're going to win the day, boys, where the Fraser River flows.[119]

The designation of Mark's book as the best thing since sliced aristocrats when it comes to the giant of early anarchism comes from Paul McLaughlin, despite the fact that he has also written a book about Bakunin in the English language.

But Mark's not even the first Vancouver author to produce a defining work of anarchist history and theory; George Woodcock's *Anarchism: A History of Libertarian Ideas and Movements,* became a touchstone for the new left internationally. Woodcock was born in Canada but raised in England, where he had worked throughout the 1930s with other anti-authoritarian leftists like George Orwell, about whose work he later wrote another celebrated book, *The Crystal Spirit.* Woodcock was "in his mid-forties when he finally settled for good in his beloved Vancouver," as the back cover copy of George Fetherling's biography of Woodcock, *The Gentle Anarchist*, puts it. Fetherling's work examines, among other things, Woodcock's processes of reinventing himself in new places; the biographer surmises that Woodcock's new home (he travelled widely, but lived in Vancouver until his death in 1995, at age eighty-three) was anything but incidental in his discovering an increased confidence in identifying as an anarchist: "He began calling himself first a philosophical anarchist and, later, once again answered to the simple title of anarchist, without qualification or modifiers. In this, he was influenced by the sense of regional identity he felt as a British Columbian [...]"[120]

In the early 1900s, the anarchist tendency in the left and labour movements was the only one to confront a Vancouver economy fractured by craft and race by proposing a universalist industrial unionism not only committed to anti-racism but also composed of a mixed membership and leadership. As historian Rolf Knight explains, though the majority of the anarcho-syndicalist Lumber

Handler's union, Local 526 of the Industrial Workers of the World (IWW), founded in 1906, were Squamish Indians, the "union included Englishmen, Hawaiians" and was co-founded by "a black Barbadian" named John St John.[121] Four years later, the IWW led a strike of predominantly Italian excavators, and at one point, the union even organized a "Russian-language branch" for Vancouver.[122]

In 1912, the IWW and its members were banned by city council from delivering their trademarked (well, not likely trademarked; in fact, *emphatically* open source) speeches at the Powell Street Grounds, today's Oppenheimer Park, named for just the sort of capitalist that the Wobblies were locked in pitched battle with. In light of the 2009 war of words between the BC Civil Liberties Association head David Eby and former Communist, now nominal social-democratic Vision Vancouver city councillor Geoff Meggs (who nevertheless seems to have retained a Soviet approach to freedom of expression) over the notorious free speech zones of the 2010 Winter Olympics, the experience of the Wobblies in 1912 is stirring and dramatic and profoundly relevant. Rather than accepting the city's decision, the IWW encouraged its members from up and down the West Coast (which had seen similar bans, as well as similar anarchist counteroffensives, all the way down to San Diego) to give public speeches in Vancouver—including from boats in the Burrard Inlet—and to overwhelm the resources of the city by getting so many people arrested that the authorities were forced to choose between bankruptcy and free speech.[123] They chose the latter (although, given what the Olympics have done to the city's coffers, the result of the contemporary stand-off might be both tyranny *and* bankruptcy).

Vanarchism went from the rough, populist anarcho-syndical-ism of the Wobblies to the gentle, and genteel, intellectual anarchism of George Woodcock, to something altogether different in the 1970s and '80s. Publications like *Open Road* were insouciant, irreverent works of anti-patriarchal, anti-nuclear, and ecologically minded anarchism, which found musical expression in the works of groups like D.O.A. and the Subhumans. The ideals of feminist, anti-war, and ecological anarchism also found expression in the dramatic, direct-action sabotage of the Vancouver Five. Though some have identified their acts with the notion of propaganda of the deed (which was certainly a part of it), the designation isn't apt because each of the actions was also a self-contained act of practical sabotage to a specific end (for example, preventing the substation or the renewal of the cruise missile contract). In retrospect, even if we condemn their violence, almost all of the actions of the Vancouver Five, in their motivation and political inclination if not their execution, can be morally reclaimed by the Left. (The exception to this might be the burning down of the porn stores, which seems decidedly anachronistic and puritanical by today's standards outside of the anti-porn feminism of sex-trade abolitionists such as Rape Relief. But that having been said, the Red Hot shops were targeted for their purveyance of especially violent pornography.)[124] The cultural scene that helped produce the Vancouver Five also rallied around them. D.O.A. put out a cover of the Subhumans' song "Fuck You"—a song that writer Grant Shilling called "non-negotiable, nihilistic and knowing [...] the essence of punk"—as part of the defence campaign.[125]

When I was a teenager years later, a new punk scene emerged, centred around Lynn Valley in North Vancouver, and I attended benefit concerts there for the Native Sundancers sieged by police and military at Gustafsen Lake in 1995 that featured local groups like Manner Farm along with Winnipeg's Propagandhi. That was just a short time before Vanarchism underwent another rebirth at the infamous APEC summit held in Vancouver and on the UBC Endowment Lands in 1998. A great deal of the opposition to the summit was organized by anarchists, including Jaggi Singh, who was preventatively detained under the bogus pretext of having assaulted a security guard's ear drums by screaming through a megaphone; it later came out that the RCMP had planned to trump up a charge to remove Singh from the action so that he couldn't participate.[126] I spent a good part of my adolescence working with Singh on actions opposing the occupation of East Timor; he brought my friends and me some picket signs for a school walk-out we organized in solidarity with the East Timorese on International Human Rights Day, after which my high school vice principal told me that Jaggi was an outside agitator. (Contrary to what this phrase would seem to indicate, I did not go to school during the Eisenhower administration, and my vice principal was not J. Edgar Hoover.) The police riot at APEC and Prime Minister Chrétien's callous indifference—"I put pepper on my plate"—galvanized and radicalized a whole layer of Vancouver activists that went on to participate in the Battle of Seattle against the World Trade Organization in 1999.

After the election of premier Gordon Campbell in 2001, the mainline progressives of the labour and social democratic movements were left reeling (in fact, "Left Reeling" could have been the headline), and the only folks who hit the ground running were the anarchists of the Anti-Poverty Committee who, though they've since been reduced by the media to nihilistic bogeymen hell-bent on destruction, carried out some of the most creative and compelling actions against the new government. These actions included their leadership role in the 100-day squat of the Woodward's building in 2002, which helped to bring down a (admittedly imploding) right-wing civic government. Although the APC was rent by a bizarro split, many of the veterans of these campaigns, as well as vestiges of the old outfit, went on to lead much of the opposition to the 2010 Winter Games in co-operation with Native activists.

It's tempting to speculate on why Vancouver hosts such a thriving anarchist tradition (Montréal and Winnipeg are really the only Canadian cities to even come close). The early economic history of the city, as the nucleus of a scattered and seasonal resources-based economy that relied on an ethnically diverse, transient, and migrant labour force, meant that the traditional craft labour movement was paralyzed either from atomization by trade or else poisonous racial paranoia. In this environment, it makes sense that outfits like the IWW would thrive. But that economy had changed quite significantly by the times of George Woodcock or Ann Hansen of the Wimmin's Fire Brigade or Jaggi Singh.

One can look to nature for at least part of the explanation as to why anarchism seems to thrive in Vancouver. The natural freedom espoused by anarchists in the tradition of Rousseau chokes without the oxygen—literal and figurative—of triumphant nature. In Vancouver, the bankers' tallest skyscrapers still look small next to the mountains, which leaves some hope. *In the Skin of a Lion*, which ends with a resignation to the new, capitalist city, could never have been set in Vancouver because its plot revolves around battles between capital and nature in a war that capital wins: dynamite in a river; a bridge over a chasm; a tunnel under a lake; the final surrender in an ornate and beautiful water-filtration plant, a man-made edifice that takes nature and makes it better.

The flourishing of anti-authoritarianism could also be the byproduct of Vancouver's dreaded marginality. A marginality in which the sense of being on-the-periphery that's so frustrating for the authors, artists, and performers who have to start again from nothing the second they cross the Rockies, or voters who feel like all they can do is register a token dissatisfaction with the electoral choices of central Canada, turns itself inside-out, and becomes a liberation.[127] If our relationship to the concentration of cultural, economic, and political power in the middle of the country is mostly ephemeral, then that cuts both ways. The less you feel like it's looking out for you, the less inclined you are to look out for it, and the narrative, emotive pull of the hegemon loses some of its power. Instead, we send our musicians back to Toronto for talk shows, and let the hosts try to figure out a way to get around saying the word "shithead." As nice and as funny as he is, you know that Mike Bullard used to be a cop, right?

Conclusion

As I type the concluding essay to this book about my city, I'm sitting on a Montréal-bound train, having just left Toronto. I'm back East to represent Vancouver in the Just For Laughs festival's Homegrown Comic Competition, and, continuing a Vancouver tradition, I've done well but haven't won (although this year's winner, Mark Little of Halifax, grew up in the Lower Mainland and used to work with me at SFU's student newspaper).

Here between these two Great Cities once pregnant with Canadian history (and now practically menopausal), it's easy to see just how marginal Vancouver is to the rest of Canada, how remote it must seem to the millions and millions of people who go about their everyday chores and joys without thinking about the port city out West, except when they want to spit expletives about the snow. Even the names of the cities are heavier, more central, more Canadian; Vancouver seems lighter, cleaner Old England, sure, but rinsed in the Pacific. When the tiny proto-city on the Burrard Inlet went from being called Gastown to Granville to, finally, Vancouver, the name was perfectly apt. Although Captain Vancouver, coming from England, was in the proper sense a Transatlantic figure, he was just as much a product of the Pacific, poking in at Canada from the West rather than trundling through from the East, weighed down with the history and prejudices and particular avarices of Ontario and Québec.

Travelling through this country, it's easy to get the impression that the city of Vancouver—where no one gets self-righteous if you want Starbucks instead of Tim Hortons, where no one has lost the bottom third of their car to hungry road salt—is the least Canadian of the country's cities. The constructed environments of most places in Canada are, materially, of a sturdier epoch: Maritime clapboard houses, Central Canadian brick apartments, faded Prairie grain elevators or Albertan oil-industry office towers. Recently, a Québécoise friend reflected admiringly of her first trip to Vancouver that *"on dirait que c'est comme une ville complètement en verre."* I told her that she had just spontaneously translated an exquisite phrase from one of Vancouver's sharpest observers, Douglas Coupland, who described Vancouver as a "City of Glass," a nearly perfect summary of both the physical city as well as what Coupland sees as its subtle, nascent identity. It's also the title he gave his incredible ABC book of Vancouver (and now that we're near the end of my book, I don't mind telling you that you should have started with his—unless you bought this from a store with a generous exchange policy, in which case disregard what I just wrote or spill some coffee, pronto).

Looking at a map of the country, Vancouver is almost comically peripheral, perched away from its countrymen on the outermost edge of the landmass like a religious girl on a couch with a boy. "Less, perhaps, than any other Canadian city Vancouver feels itself a part of Canada," wrote the then-editor of the *Vancouver Sun*, Bruce Hutchison, in his 1950 book, *The Fraser*. And yet there's still a family resemblance. In his essay "British Columbia: What Did You Expect?" George Bowering pointed up the irony of Canadian nationalists in Toronto complaining about American imperialism—while at the same time marginalizing the West—by calling British Columbians "the Canadians of Canada."[128] In a similar vein, though it may be the least Canadian city in the country, Vancouver is in many ways the city most *like* Canada: vacillating wildly between a strong inferiority complex and intense narcissism; celebrating its abundance of natural beauty but bristling whenever outsiders try to reduce it to nature exclusively; juggling a mixed, pre- and post-modern economy of natural resource extraction, service, hi-tech, and culture alongside anaemic heavy industry; building a young, multicultural settler society amidst the partial ruins and partial renaissances of ancient indigenous ones. As the world economy and international culture continue along the slow, painful shift from an emphasis on the Transatlantic to an emphasis on the Transpacific, the example set by Vancouver as well as the existing cultural and economic connections that already exist here will become increasingly important to the country as a whole. Calgary and Vancouver could very well be the Toronto and Montréal of the next century.

One of the observations you sometimes hear or read in interviews with Coupland is a variation on the theme that, while other cities are already what they are, Vancouver is still becoming what it's going to be, and that that's more exciting. It's a characteristically optimistic prognosis, though I think that Vancouver's identity is a lot more fixed and established than Coupland and many others give it credit for being. Hutchison's book on the city, written nearly sixty years ago, makes these observations:

In spring you may pick roses on the warm riverbank
and half an hour later ski in the mountain snow [...]
Vancouver is casual, unconventional, untidy, and not too
carefully dressed as compared with the older cities of the
East [...] On the top Vancouver is ruled by the most garish
tycoons to date in Canada [...] In the shelter of this mushroom aristocracy, and usually with the aid of its campaign
funds, Vancouver has produced some of the worst politics
in Canada [...] At the other extreme Vancouver is a labour
town of powerful unions [...] No Eastern influence, but
the presence of the forest and the ocean, has moulded the
city's character, made its inhabitants an outdoor, athletic,
gardening, boat-loving, easygoing people.[129]

Editing only for style, Hutchison could write those same sentiments today; in fact, most of those observations have become
clichés. (Note: you may also want to edit Hutchison for racism, as in
this gem: "The first Indian inhabitants of the [Fraser] river region,
near the coast, were among the least energetic in America, soft only
in their speech and stern only in their aversion to labour. It has
always been a favourite theory of mine that in time the coast will
make the white man like the Indian. I could point out to any interested investigator a good many specimens to prove my point."[130] Oh,
Bruce! You and your theorem! From drugs to free-speech politics
to the relationship with nature, the more one looks at Vancouver's
history, the more one sees that many of its traits seem to have been
integrated from the beginning.

This is not to say that Vancouver isn't in the process of deciding what kind of city it's going to be, decisions that are becoming
more and more difficult to approach blindly. Are we going to be a
resort town for the super-rich from all around the world, or a functional, integrated city? An outpost of America's shitty and dying
film and television industries, or a thriving centre of authentic
cultural exchange? Will we treat the immiseration of our poorest
and most vulnerable citizens as an opportunity for creative social
policy or creative real estate speculation? Will we be a green beacon
of rational, ecological planning, or a capital of corporate green-
washing and weak-kneed political tokenism? A sad, gang-riddled
microcosm of the War on Drugs, or a leader in addiction treatment

(not to mention a fun, civilized place to be, with revenues from taxing the best weed in the world)? A surveillance state, replete with wild abuses of police powers, or a relatively free society?

Each of these fundamental questions about the nature of Vancouver is—in relation to policy actively being made—on the table. And, as even greater cause for optimism, the neo-liberal pseudo-philosophies of the past several decades, which have left cities (just like ours) choked and paralyzed and ever more inclined towards mean-spiritedness, are finally losing their lustre. For the first time in years, some Vancouverites are willing to admit that betting an entire economy on the guaranteed exponential increases in value of a $700,000 one-bedroom condo in an algae-streaked building on a major seismic fault line may not, in fact, be the most sane way of doing things.

Looking at the civic politics and policy that arose in the wake of Expo 86 leading up to the Olympics, it's easy to get the impression that Vancouver refuses to learn from history. But much of the community organizing against the excesses and cruelties of the 2010 Games drew upon the lessons of Expo 86, which drew upon the stubborn refusal of East End communities to give up their homes for highways in the 1960s and '70s, which drew upon the millions of stories of the resistance and scepticism of regular people to the encroachments of speculators and developers going all the way back to 1865, when the Indians at Whoi Whoi gave the stink eye to a colonial surveyor.[131] There are rich legacies of both good and bad decisions here, positive and negative social traditions we perpetuate. In that sense, we're just like any other city.

Only we don't get any snow here. Oh, and we have the mountains.

NOTES

Introduction

1. Sean Condon, "Time Travel: Vancouver 1980," Only (April 15, 2008), *http://onlymagazine.net/City/2119/time-travel-vancouver-1980*.

2. Mark Leier, *Red Flags and Red Tape: The Making of a Labour Bureaucracy* (Toronto: University of Toronto Press, 1995).

3. Ibid., 44.

4. George Bowering, *Burning Water* (Vancouver: New Star Books, 2007), 141.

Commercial Drive

5. Bruce Serafin, *Colin's Big Thing* (Victoria, BC: Ekstasis Editions, 2003), 248.

Robson Street

6. *City Reflections*, DVD (1907, 2008; Vancouver: Vancouver Historical Society).

7. Peter Miller, "The Manhattan; A Once Doomed Building is Reborn," the Province (September 4, 1983), *http://vcn.bc.ca/man/history.html*.

Chinatown

8. Wayson Choy, *The Jade Peony* (Vancouver: Douglas & McIntyre, 1995), 10.

9. Frances Bula, "Mere suggestion of towers in Chinatown brings out the forces," State of Vancouver (May 12, 2009), *http://www./francesbula.com/?p=1589*.

10. Wayde Compton, *Performance Bond* (Vancouver: Arsenal Pulp Press, 2004).

Kitsilano

11. The Naam, *http://www.thenaam.com*.

12. Rex Weyler, *Greenpeace* (Vancouver: Raincoast Books, 2005), 48.

13. Bruce Serafin, *Stardust* (Vancouver: New Star Books, 2007), 60.

14. Craigslist, *http://vancouver.fr.craigslist.ca/cas/1270424533.html*.

Main Street

15. Douglas Haddow, "Hipster: The Dead End of Western Civilization," *Adbusters* (July 2008), *http://adbusters.org/magazine/79/hipster.html*.

16. "Exhausting the Adbusters Hipster Article," We Hate Vancouver (September 25, 2008), *http://wehatevancouver.blogspot.com/2008/09/exhausting-adbusters-hipster-article.html*, and "Hipsters Are Not a Crime," Beyond Robson (July 30, 2008), *http://beyondrobson.com/fashion/2008/07/hipsters_are_not_a_crime/*.

Davie Village

17. Ben Swanky, *COPE 1968–1993: Working for Vancouver*.

18. Bruce Macdonald, *Vancouver: A Visual History* (Vancouver: Talonbooks, 1998).

19. Ibid.

20. Ibid., 32.

Downtown Eastside

21. Past Tense Vancouver, *http://pasttensevancouver.wordpress.com/*.

22. Jeff Sommers and Nick Blomley, "The Worst Block in Vancouver," in Stan Douglas, *Every Building on 100 West Hastings Street* (Vancouver: Arsenal Pulp Press and Contemporary Art Gallery, 2002), 50.

23. "The Dope Craze That's Terrorizing Vancouver," Past Tense Vancouver (August 3, 2008), *http://pasttensevancouver.wordpress.com/2008/08/03/"the-dope-craze-that's-terrorizing-vancouver"/*.

24. Ibid.

25. Transcript of negotiations discussion (12/12), *West Coast Line*, 41, Fall/Winter 2003–2004, 175:

26. Ibid., 91.

27. Sommers and Blomley, 53.

On the Waterfronts

28. Sommers and Blomley, 18–58.

29. "mylosh" at Flickr, *http://www.flickr.com/photos/mylosh/403205398/*.

30. Mike Harcourt and Ken Cameron with Sean Rossiter, *City Making in Paradise* (Vancouver: Douglas & McIntyre, 2007), 100–101.

31. Ibid., 99.

32. Matt Hearn, "No Recipe for Funk," *Vancouver Review*, Spring 2008.

33. For more on this formula and the development of False Creek, see the chapter "Expo 86 and the Remaking of False Creek" in *City Making in Paradise*.

Suburbs

34. Daniel Francis, *L.D.: Mayor Louis Taylor and the Rise of Vancouver* (Vancouver: Arsenal Pulp Press, 2004), 75.

35. Ben Swanky, *1968–1993 COPE*, 17.

First Nations

36. Bruce Macdonald, *Vancouver*, 41.

37. Rolf Knight, *Indians at Work: An Informal History of Native Indian Labour in British Columbia 1858–1930*, 2nd ed. (Vancouver: New Star Books, 1996), 247.

38. Ibid., 247–48.

39. Earle Birney, "The Speech of the Salish Chief" from *The Damnation of Vancouver*, collected in *One Muddy Hand: Selected Poems* (Madeira Park, BC: Harbour Publishing, 2006), 71.

40. Jean Barman, *Stanley Park's Secret* (Madeira Park, BC: Harbour Publishing, 2005), 13.

41. Ibid., 61–62.

42. Macdonald, *Vancouver*, 17.

43. Robin Laurence, "Introduction" in E. Pauline Johnson, *Legends of Vancouver* (Vancouver: Douglas & McIntyre, 1998), xv.

44. Ibid.

45. Eden Robinson, *Traplines* (New York: Henry Holt and Company, 1996), 35.

46. Lee Maracle, "Polka Partners, Uptown Indians and White Folks," in *The Vancouver Stories: West Coast Fiction from Canada's Best Writers* (Vancouver: Raincoast Books, 2005).

Québécois

47. Normand Lester, *Le Livre Noir Du Canada Anglais 2*, 277–278.

48. René Lévesque, The Snare of Biculturalism, in *An Option for Quebec* (Toronto: McClelland & Stewart, 1968).

Celebrities

49. "Errol Flynn" on Wikipedia, *http://en.wikipedia.org/wiki/Errol_Flynn#Death*.

50. Daniel Francis, *Red Light Neon: A History of Vancouver's Sex Trade* (Vancouver: Subway Books, 1996), 87–88.

51. Guy Macpherson, "Dane Cook Gets the Hook at Yuk Yuk's," the *Province*, July 25, 2006.

Black History

52. Statistics from Statistics Canada, cited in Samantha Amara and Beverly Cramp, *The Vancouver Book of Everything* (Lunenburg, NS: MacIntyre Purcell Publishing, 2008), 84–89.

53. Statistics Canada, "2006 Community Profiles," *http://www12.statcan.gc.ca/census-recensement/2006/dp-pd/prof/92-591*.

54. Adam Julian Rudder, "A Black Community in Vancouver?: A History of Invisibility (masters thesis, University of Victoria, BC, 2004), 1. *http://hdl.handle.net/1828/733*.

55. Ibid.

56. Lani Russwurm, "If It Ain't Got That Swing," Past Tense Vancouver, *http://pasttensevancouver.wordpress.com/2008/12/10/if-it-aint-got-that-swing*.

57. Macdonald, *Vancouver*, 60–61, and also "Brown, Rosemary," *http://fcis.oise.utoronto.ca/~gpieters/brownbio.html*.

58. Macdonald, *Vancouver*, 61.

Police

59. Leigh Kamping-Carder, "At the Gastown Riot," *The Walrus*, July/August 2009.

60. *The Police and the Community: Implications of the Report of the Commission of Enquiry by Mr. Justice Dohm*, BC Civil Liberties Association, Position Paper, 1971, *http://www.bccla.org/positions/police/71community.html*.

61. Matthew Burrows, "Police Still Rogues, Louis Charges," *Georgia Straight* (April 13, 2006), *http://www.straight.com/article/police-still-rogues-louis-charges*.

Rich People

62. Lance Berelowitz, *Dream City: Vancouver and the Global Imagination* (Vancouver: Douglas & McIntyre, 2005), 97.

63. Bruce Serafin, *Stardust*, 5.

64. "The Fraser Institute at 30," CBC News Online (October 12, 2004), *http://www.cbc.ca/news/background/fraserinstitute*.

Nature

65. Geoff Dembicki, "Vancouver's 'Brand': Ski Bums or Green Brainiacs?", the *Tyee* (July 27, 2009), *http://thetyee.ca/News/2009/07/27/VancouverBrand/*.

66. E. Pauline Johnson, "The Two Sisters," *Legends of Vancouver*, 1.

67. Mahmoud Darwish, "Poem of the Land," in Salma Khadra Jayyusi, ed., *Anthology of Modern Palestinian Literature* (Irvington, NY: Columbia University Press, 1994), 146.

68. Lance Berelowitz, *Dream City*, 9.

Pot

69. Todd S. Purdom, "It Came from Wasilla," *Vanity Fair* (August 2009), *http://www.vanityfair.com/politics/features/2009/08/sarah-palin200908?printable=true&currentPage=all*.

Crime

70. Lani Russwurm, "Clearing Hastings Townsite," Past Tense Vancouver, *http://pasttensevancouver.wordpress.com/2008/09/12/clearing-hastings-townsite*.

71. Lani Russwurm, "What Frankie Said," Past Tense Vancouver, *http://pasttensevancouver.wordpress.com/2008/12/29/what-frankie-said*.

72. Misha Glenny, *McMafia: A Journey Through the Global Criminal Underworld* (Toronto: Anansi, 2009), 230.

73. "British Columbia or Colombia," the *Economist* (May 28, 2009), *http://www.economist.com/world/americas/displaystory.cfm?story_id=13740305*.

74. Daniel Francis, *Red Light Neon*, 51.

75. Lani Russwurm, "The Dope Craze That's Terrorizing Vancouver."

Peace

76. Lance Berelowitz, *Dream City*, 138.

77. "1918," The History of Metropolitan Vancouver, *http://www.vancouverhistory.ca/chronology1918.htm*.

78. Mark Leier, *Rebel Life: The Life and Times of Robert Gosden, Revolutionary, Mystic, Labour Spy* (Vancouver: New Star Books, 1999), 76–77. 79. "1918."

80. Weyler, Rex, "Vancouver Loves Peace," *Common Ground* (May 2006), *http://www.commonground.ca/iss/0605178/cg178_peace.shtml*.

81. Frank Kennedy, "Vancouver

Responds," Letter, *Peace Calendar* vol. 2 no. 7 (August 1984), *http://www. peacemagazine.org/peacecalendar/tpc-v2n07.html.*

82. Ben Swanky, *1968–1993 COPE*, 212.

83. Claire Perry, "U.S. Destroyers Drop Anchor as Thousands March for Peace," *Peace Magazine*, (June/July 1987), *http:// archive.peacemagazine.org/v03n3p40.htm.*

Municipal Politics

84. Nathan Allan, "The Enemy of Their Emerson is Our Friend," Us on Them (February 12, 2006), *http://usonthem.blogsome. com/2006/02.*

85. Daniel Francis, *L.D.*, 202.

86. Ibid., 198.

87. Ben Swanky, *1968–1993 COPE*, 2.

88. Ibid., i.

89. Mark Leier, *Red Flags and Red Tape*, 59.

90. Ben Swanky, *1968–1993 COPE*, 74.

91. Charles Demers, "Cadman can end the crisis," *Georgia Straight* (May 10, 2007), *http://straight.com/article-90262/david-cadman-can-end-the-crisis.*

Moving Around

92. Ben Swanky, *1968–1993 COPE*, 32–33.

93. *City Reflections* DVD.

94. Ibid.

95. Harcourt, et al., *City Making in Paradise*, 94.

96. Tim Falconer, *Drive* (Toronto: Viking Canada, 2008), 3–4.

97. Tim Falconer, "Autoholics," *This Magazine* (March/April 2009), *http:// www.thismagazine.ca/issues/2009/03/ autoholics.php.*

98. David Beers, "Want One Port Mann Bridge or a Light Rail Metropolis?" the *Tyee* (March 25, 2009), *http://thetyee.ca/ News/2009/03/25/LightRail.*

99. David Beers, "A Prius for Every Student," the *Tyee* (December 16, 2008), *http://thetyee.ca/Views/2008/12/16/Prius.*

Food

100. "Canuck claims kudos on TV's Iron Chef America," (February 21, 2005), *http://www.ctv.ca/servlet/ArticleNews/ story/CTVNews/1109021886729_4%3Fhub= Entertainment.*

Racism

101. Joy Kogawa, *Obasan* (Toronto: Penguin Canada, 2006), 2.

102. Mark Leier, *Rebel Life*.

103. Norman Buchignani, *Continuous Journey* (Toronto: McClelland & Stewart, 1985).

104. Tom Sandborn, "Labour Double-Standards Blamed for Farmworkers' Deaths," the *Tyee* (March 16, 2007), *http:// thetyee.ca/News/2007/03/16/Farmworkers.*

105. Paul Yee, *Saltwater City: An Illustrated History of the Chinese in Vancouver* (Vancouver: Douglas & McIntyre, 2006), 57.

106. Ibid., 86.

107. Ibid.

108. Paul Delany, ed. *Vancouver: Representing the Postmodern City* (Vancouver: Arsenal Pulp Press, 1994).

Homes

109. Lani Russwurm, "A Menace to Society," Past Tense Vancouver (July 16, 2009), *http://pasttensevancouver.wordpress. com/2009/07/16/a-menace-to-society.*

110. "Stunning Increase in Number of Greater Vancouver Homeless," the *Province* (September 17, 2008), *http:// www.canada.com/theprovince/news/ story.html?id=12d1dfbd-1395-490c-836e-4ba794c7167f.*

111. British Columbia. Legislative Assembly. *Debates and Proceedings (Hansard).* 38th Legislature, 5th Session, vol. 41, no. 3 (March 26, 2009), *http://www.leg.bc.ca/ HANSARD/38th5th/h90326p.htm.*

Hollywood North

112. "Catch and Release," Internet Movie Database, *http://www.imdb.com/title/ tt0395495/goofs.*

113. Paul Delany, *Vancouver: Representing the Postmodern City.*

114. Ibid.

115. "The Last Airpuncher," FilmDrunk, *http://filmdrunk.uproxx.com/2009/07/the-last-airpuncher-the-interview.*

Sports

116. Ethan Trex, "What Your Favourite Teams Were Almost Called," *Wall Street Journal* (June 3, 2009), *http://online.wsj. com/article/SB124346122030959951.html.*

Vanarchism

117. Bob Sarti, "Open Road," in *Only a Beginning: An Anarchist Anthology*, ed. Allan Antliff (Vancouver: Arsenal Pulp Press, 2004), 9–10.

118. Grant Shilling, "We Don't Care What You Say," *Broken Pencil* [n.d.], *http:// www.brokenpencil.com/features/feature. php?featureid=47.*

119. Joe Hill, "Where the Fraser River Flows," reprinted in Leier, *Where the Fraser River Flows.*

120. Fetherling, George, *The Gentle Anarchist: A Life of George Woodcock* (Vancouver: Douglas & McIntyre, 1998), 99.

121. Rolf Knight, *Indians at Work* (Vancouver: New Star Books, 1998), 247.

122. Mark Leier, *Where the Fraser River Flows*, 43.

123. For the best accounts of Vancouver's 1912 free-speech fight, see Mark Leier's lecture "Historical Snapshots North of the Border," available online at *http://www. youtube.com/watch?v=MiTcj8UlS2U* as well as his book *Rebel Life*; my summary of these events is greatly indebted to both.

124. Jim Campbell, "From Protest to Resistance: the Vancouver Five Remembered," in *Only a Beginning.*

125. Grant Shilling, "We Don't Care What You Say."

126. "Crown Drops Charge Against APEC Protesters," CBC News (February 12, 1999), *http://www.cbc.ca/canada/ story/1999/02/01/singh990201.html.*

127. For the best description of this frustration, see George Bowering's essay "British Columbia: What Did You Expect?" *Left Hook* (Vancouver: Raincoast Books, 2005).

Conclusion

128. George Bowering, *Left Hook*, 55.

129. Bruce Hutchison, *The Fraser* (Toronto: Clarke, Irwin, 1965, 1950), 170–173.

130. Ibid.

131. See Jean Barman, *Stanley Park's Secret*, 32.

FURTHER READING

Barman, Jean. *Stanley Park's Secret: The Forgotten Families of Whoi Whoi, Kanaka Ranch, and Brockton Point.* Madeira Park, BC: Harbour Publishing, 2005.

Berelowitz, Lance. *Dream City: Vancouver and the Global Imagination.* Vancouver: Douglas & McIntyre, 2005.

Bowering, George. *Burning Water.* Vancouver: New Star Books, 2007.

Choy, Wayson. *The Jade Peony.* Vancouver: Douglas & McIntyre, 1995.

Compton, Wayde. *Performance Bond.* Vancouver: Arsenal Pulp Press, 2004.

Coupland, Douglas. *City of Glass.* Vancouver: Douglas & McIntyre, 2000.

Delany, Paul (ed). *Vancouver: Representing the Postmodern City.* Vancouver: Arsenal Pulp Press, 1994.

Douglas, Stan. *Every Building on 100 West Hastings Street.* Vancouver: Arsenal Pulp Press and Contemporary Art Gallery, 2002.

Fetherling, George. *The Gentle Anarchist.* Vancouver: Douglas & McIntyre, 1998.

Francis, Daniel. *L.D.: Mayor Louis Taylor and the Rise of Vancouver.* Vancouver: Arsenal Pulp Press, 2004.

—— *Red Light Neon: A History of Vancouver's Sex Trade.* Vancouver: Subway Books, 1996.

Harcourt, Mike, Ken Cameron, and Sean Rossiter. *City Making in Paradise: Nine Decisions That Saved Vancouver.* Vancouver: Douglas & McIntyre, 2007.

Hutchison, Bruce. *The Fraser.* Toronto: Clarke, Irwin, 1982, © 1950.

Johnson, E. Pauline. *Legends of Vancouver.* Vancouver: Douglas & McIntyre, 1998.

Knight, Rolf. *Indians at Work*: *An Informal History of Native Indian Labour in British Columbia 1858–1930,* 2nd ed. Vancouver: New Star Books, 1996.

Kogawa, Joy. *Obasan.* Toronto: Penguin Canada, 2006.

Lee, Jen Sookfong. *The End of East.* Toronto: A.A. Knopf Canada, 2007.

Leier, Mark. *Red Flags and Red Tape: The Making of a Labour Bureaucracy.* Toronto: University of Toronto Press, 1995.

—— *Rebel Life: The Life and Times of Robert Gosden, Revolutionary, Mystic, Labour Spy.* Vancouver: New Star Books, 1999.

—— *Where the Fraser River Flows: The Industrial Workers of the World in British Columbia.* Vancouver: New Star Books, 1990.

Macdonald, Bruce. *Vancouver: A Visual History.* Vancouver: Talonbooks, 1992.

Stanley, George. *Vancouver: A Poem.* Vancouver: New Star Books, 2008.

Yee, Paul. *Saltwater City: An Illustrated History of the Chinese in Vancouver.* Vancouver: Douglas & McIntyre, 1988.

The Vancouver Stories: West Coast Fiction from Canada's Best Writers. Vancouver: Raincoast Books, 2005.

INDEX

Charles Demers was born and raised in Vancouver. He is an activist and comedian, a regular performer on CBC Radio One's The Debaters, and co-host of Citytv's comedic panel show The Citynews List in Vancouver.

In 2005, he was the judges' choice for Vancouver's funniest new comic; since then he has been featured on national radio, in print, as well as in festivals and live venues across Canada and the Pacific Northwest and with Paul Bae as the sketch duo "Bucket" the act Robin Williams called "the future of comedy." His first novel, *The Prescription Errors*, was published in fall 2009 by Insomniac Press.

Photo: Dennis Whitfield